Ten Natural Steps to Training the Family Dog

Building a Positive Relationship

Matthew Duffy

ISBN: 1456526308
ISBN 13: 9781456526306

"On the way, the queen and four of the brothers died; they were not sufficiently pure to be able to enter heaven in their human bodies. Only Yudhisthira, the royal saint, journeyed on, accompanied by his faithful dog. When they reached heaven, Indra, the king of gods, told him that the dog could not come in. Yudhisthira replied that, if this were so, he would stay outside heaven too, but he could not bring himself to desert any creature which trusted him and wished for his protection. Finally, after a long argument, both the dog and king were admitted. Then the dog was revealed as Dharma himself. This had been yet another test of Yudhisthira's spiritual greatness."

—*Bhagavad-Gita*, circa 300 BC

Dedication

To Mother Nature,
Who taught me about Spirit

Contents

Biography

Matthew Duffy was born and raised in southern Indiana, the beautiful hilly country overlooking the mighty Ohio River. His natural rapport with animals became apparent at the young age of thirteen when Matt worked as a mounted trail guide for a local riding stable. After years of working with horses, Matt turned his full attention to dogs. He completed a comprehensive professional dog trainer's course in 1980 and soon became the head trainer at a prominent kennel in Louisville, Kentucky. In 1983, Matt entered into a partnership with a dog training center in Indiana and several years later established his own training facility, Advanced Training Kennel, Inc.

During Matt's very active career, he has:

- titled dogs to various levels of working degrees, while a member of the United Schutzhund Clubs of America;

- completed courses at the Koehler Method of Dog Training Clinic, the International Police Dogs (scent detection) seminar, the All Breed K-9 Academy (patrol dog) seminar, and the Tom Brown Tracking School;

- studied psychology at Indiana University Southeast and was inducted into the National Honor Society in Psychology in 1983;

- graduated from the Floyd County Police Academy and served as a K-9 officer;

- been an active member of the North American Police Work Dog Association and the Indiana Search and Rescue Work Dog Association.

Currently, Matt owns and operates Duffy's Dog Training Center LLC, where he oversees the instruction of several hundred dogs and their owners annually. A master of his trade, Matthew Duffy has trained literally thousands of dogs over the past two and a half decades for every imaginable purpose: family obedience, handicap assistance, search and rescue, even termite detection. Any working day of the week, you'll find Matt with a leash in his hand, ever continuing to sharpen his expertise.

Acknowledgments

Without the help of the following people, this book would have never reached fruition. It is my sincere wish that every reader spend enough time to acknowledge the names listed below; for each one of these good friends invested real thought, real time, and real effort into this project. Their support and enthusiasm, at every turn, gave me the confidence to forge ahead.

I want to thank first and foremost my associates David Benson, Kathy Pruit, and Cathy Cantu for their undying interest in this book and for their invaluable insights during countless hours of dog training discussions. They truly helped to keep me focused.

I owe much to Mitzi Streepy and her expert editing ability; she helped turn my rough manuscript into a real book, and she, above all others, made me feel that this book was worth reading.

I am deeply grateful to my two scientific friends Dr. John Parker and Karen Brinkley who so meticulously and expeditiously edited the content and structure of the manuscript. Through their expert eyes, we were able to refine the book into its finished readable form. Simply because I asked, they carried out this task with the kindness and concern of true friends. I will never forget their favor.

I also would like to thank Nolan Hulsey for his professional and patient photographic skills. His contribution to this book is priceless, and we all enjoyed his infectious enthusiasm for photography.

I must say that this project would have come to a screeching halt were it not for my son, Zachary Paul. He jumped on board when I needed help the most, putting together all the final pieces of the book. Imbedding pictures, organizing everything in proper electronic format, satisfying the demands of the publisher, and developing a marketing strategy—all these tasks combined with operating the training center created an overwhelming challenge for me. When Zachary came to my aid, he immediately stepped into the role of agent/book doctor with such ease and competence it was hard to believe he was actually a neophyte. In large part, you are able to appreciate this book because of Zachary's diligent contributions.

Just when I thought all of the tedious work was finished, the final proof readings rolled around. I needed one more set of fresh, intelligent eyes to meticulously read over every word of the manuscript. How grateful I was that my daughter, Heidi Rose, jumped on these challenge. With the Highest degree of care and comprehension, she covered this book from front to back and then from back to front, helping me with numerous clarifications and corrections. We made a good team.

Finally I would like to offer special thanks to all of our gracious clients, who allowed us to photograph their dogs and themselves during training. Without their contribution, this book would have fallen short of being the family-dog instruction manual we had intended it to be.

I am truly a fortunate man for having had the opportunity to work with my son and daughter along with so many other good people.

A Personal Introduction

I've spent my entire adult life working with dogs. Over the course of twenty-seven years, thousands of families have entrusted the training of their canine family members to me. Handling more than ten thousand family dogs has given me the unique opportunity to develop a training approach that specifically addresses the balance between a human family and its dogs.

My appreciation and acceptance of animals the way they are is a direct result of my mother's natural and insightful tutelage. Reared in the country, my mother was surrounded by animals through adolescence. Whether it was at home with her own pet crow, dog, or horse or at a best friend's house with multiple horses or a weekend on Grandmother's farm, she lived for the animals. Mother always loved animals just the way they were. She proved to be an outstanding horsewoman all her life. Equally adept at English or Western riding styles, Mom rode with passion. I had the good fortune of working with her most of my life. We managed a riding stable together during my teens, and as soon as I finished my education, she followed me into the dog training business. All through the years, Mom carried with her an amazement for people who didn't understand animals. She spent countless hours on the phone explaining to clients how to adjust their dog's behavior to suit the family routine or modify the home environment to better suit dog ownership rather than fruitlessly trying to shape a dog into a four-legged human being.

Mom succumbed to colon cancer at the age of sixty-seven. In true Shari Duffy form, she spent her last conscious moments feebly riding her beloved Connemara. It would be impossible for me to determine how much of my animal communication skill I learned or inherited from Mom, but I know it would be considerable, and I will always be deeply grateful for those many years of her teaching and company.

Given my background it's hard to imagine why anyone would want their canine companion to be anything other than the animal he is. However, it is my impression from working with many thousands of dog owners that their pet would be much easier to assimilate into the family unit if he were more human-like, more familiar, more informative, and more cooperative. That is what many pet owners want from their dogs. Unfortunately, those demands are unattainable. It is unfair to a pet to ask him to give more than he can. But when a pet cannot reach these unrealistic expectations, frustration and disappointment begin to define the relationship between the owner and the dog.

The head of the average family I deal with often falls short on enough time to comfortably manage all the aspects of pack living: too little time for the kids and spouse, even less time for himself or herself, and next to no time for the dog. In our amped-up American lifestyle, we have so much on our daily plate that there is little room left for any additional challenge, like owning a dog.

How sad it would be to miss out on such a rewarding and ancient relationship. This has been my job over the past three decades: helping families minimize the challenge of dog ownership so that it fits on their daily plate. Honestly, with a few environmental controls and the right kind of relationship development, anyone who wishes to can enjoy a canine companion as the first breeders intended: an animal uniquely developed to live among people.

As for me, my favorite pastimes of hiking and backpacking are most pleasurable with my dog, because through his eyes, ears, and nose, I more fully experience the woods, the wildlife, and the rain. I share his uninhibited excitement. When my guardian alerts on a wraith in the distance (imagined or not), I'm alert. When my hunter is on the hot trail of a deer, I'm on the trail too. When my partner is mesmerized by a fascinating scent, my experience is enhanced as well. Every morning dawns fresh and new for my German shepherd, no matter how ordinary the day might seem to me. He's my fountain of youth, and I like him just the way he is: raw, excited, and a little bit challenging.

The naturalist Euell Gibbons, in his book *Stalking the Wild Asparagus*, divulges a secret about his passion in searching for wild edibles. Although past middle age at the time of the book's publication, Euell Gibbons said, "When I am out along the hedgerows and waysides gathering wild asparagus, I am twelve years old again and the world is new and wonderful ..."

I feel much the same way whenever I turn my attention toward dogs. I am immediately whisked back to my early youth, exploring the backyard with my ninety-pound, four-legged shadow named Kaiser. He was a magnificent German shepherd my parents bought when I was two. My mother (affectionately referred to by my father as Mother Nature) knew in her heart that a firstborn child could have no better companion and guardian than a devoted shepherd. So for the next ten years, when I played army, Kaiser played army. When he dug for moles, I dug for moles. We shared lunch in his doghouse and studied each other in the shade on hot summer days. Kaiser taught me how to growl, and I taught him how to sit and shake.

He was my best friend. I was afraid of nothing when we were together. My close relationship with Kaiser enriched my childhood for sure. I learned to appreciate the outdoors, food, and activity with extraordinary gusto because of his infectious enthusiasm.

Today, I am fifty years old and not ashamed to say that when I hike in the woods with my German shepherd or have iced tea on the porch watching him chase after whatever I throw, I am the same happy boy of all those years ago.

Getting Started

Ten years ago she split the air
To seize what she could spy;
Tonight she bumps against a chair,
Betrayed by milky eye.
She seems to pant, Time up, time up!
My little dog must die,
And lie in the dust with Hector's pup;
So presently, must I.
    —Ogden Nash, Versus (1949)

What are dogs? If we should ask our clients to answer that question the first day they come to us, they might begin by talking in terms that make their family dog seem like a kind of alternate human. They generally endow their dogs with complex emotions and many times refer to their companion as "my baby." They might call themselves "Mommy" and "Daddy" when they refer to their relationship with their dog. And they often tell us that their dog understands everything they do and say.

We always listen and nod, even though it is clear at the moment that the dog does not understand *everything* or else it wouldn't be trying to bite me while the owner says, "*No, Rex!*" We find that one of the problems that make training pets challenging for their owners is that they do not really understand what their dog is and where he or she came from.

For those of us who make our living training dogs, we know dogs are very little like humans. They are dogs. They have evolved almost certainly from wolves and have become domesticated in only the last fifteen thousand years or so.

It is most helpful to our clients to understand the origins of the dog they own, the dog that they are willing to treat as a beloved member of their family. Often, the first difficulty our clients face is not understanding their pets and therefore expecting behaviors that a dog, because of what he is, cannot possibly deliver.

So where did our family dog begin to take shape? According to today's most informed archaeologists and geneticists, *Canis familiaris* was recognizable about fifteen thousand years ago. The oldest skeletal remains of a domesticated dog were unearthed in Germany and dated at fourteen thousand years ago (Nicholas Wade, "From Wolf to Dog, Yes, but When?" *New York Times*, November 22, 2002).This makes *Canis familiaris* the very first animal or plant domesticated by man.

Coincidentally, or perhaps naturally, the latest archeological discoveries point to the same time period for the first human settlements in the Near East. This time period is referred to as the Upper Paleolithic Age, which spanned from forty-five thousand to ten thousand years ago. The human family of this age relied on stone tools and had not yet developed agriculture. Although our ancestors were only in the crudest stages of settled society as we recognize it, our beloved dog was already in place.

The sudden appearance of *Canis familiaris* at this time has always been somewhat puzzling to historians because of the lack of evidence pointing to a direct ancestor. The dog didn't just pop into existence fifteen thousand years ago. But until very recently, there had been no archeological trail leading to our modern canine.

Now with the advent of mitochondrial DNA studies, geneticists are able to say with new certainty that dogs descended from wolves (Canis lupus) alone (Peter Salolainan et al., "Genetic Evidence," *Science* 2002). More surprisingly, the DNA evidence points to a small group of Asian wolves as the predecessors for all of today's domestic dogs.

From arctic Siberia, *Canis familiaris* migrated right along with people to every corner of this world. What could have possibly been so intriguing or significant about a tamed wolf companion that it would warrant a Stone Age people to launch into selective breeding and raising of countless canines for the purpose of developing a more improved version?

Here are some possibilities: The first settled people recognized the early warning potential against human invaders when they regularly witnessed the scavenging wolves around the perimeter of the settlement disperse prior to the approach of outsiders. Maybe, observing the wolves aggressively guarding carcasses or pups against intruders, the first domesticators envisioned their tagalong pack one day protecting the entire settlement the same way. Or it could have been a much more fundamental plan: A few vulnerable pups were captured and raised to be a convenient meat source.

Why was the canine the first animal to be domesticated? Why is more value placed on the dog in this contemporary period of alarm systems and security lights, firearms and police protection, available processed food, and adequate shelter and insulation?

Why did the domestic dog project prove to be so successful? Dogs spread throughout the entire world right along with the human migration. Why has the human/dog relationship endured so long? Through the process of domestication, we have not removed the animal instincts from the dog; we have only modified their basic characteristics. Clearly, the variation in physical appearance from an Asian wolf ancestor to the papillon is astounding, but in reality, we're dealing with essentially the same genetic material in both animals. Through countless generations of selective breeding (carefully choosing only the most vocal pups from each successive generation to reproduce), humans have been able to bring about a noisy version of the quiet hunter, yet the hunter remains.

The defining three characteristics that separate *Canis familiaris* from *Canis lupus* are the most sought-after traits in today's family dogs: tractability (docility along with the ability to read human signals), smaller, more manageable size (in regards to harboring, maintaining, and transporting), and barking (alarm, defense, and signaling). In fact, the only thing that seems to have changed over our fifteen-thousand-year relationship with the dog is the priority assigned to any one of these three characteristics.

Maybe the answer to all four questions is the same simple response: fondness!

That would explain why in the poorest of today's cultures, dogs don't hold much value (the very cultures that lack in alarm and protection capabilities, that lack in available processed food, that lack in adequate shelter and insulation).

In modern times, dogs are definitely a luxury more than any kind of necessity. Maybe it has always been that way! Maybe it's always been the luxury of companionship that grew out of fondness. (I've noticed a trend over the last three decades as the number of children in the average Midwestern family decreases, the number of dogs in that family seems to increase.) The companionship was primary; the barking and food source was secondary.

To be truly comfortable living in close quarters with a family dog, we must be prepared to appreciate him for what he is, an animal—an animal, to be sure, which has proven to be marvelously adaptable and uniquely qualified for the tasks we set for him. Trouble will surely arise between owner and dog if the owner is not able to accept this truth.

At least fifteen millennia have passed since man and dog forged their unique relationship. Like no other animal, *Canis familiaris* has fully adapted to the hominid way. Our domestic friend is quite comfortable in the thick of the human condition, and we have learned to communicate with each other in an extraordinary fashion. The family dog can comfortably interchange people with members of his own species when identifying the pack, subjecting all equally to the rules of canine interaction.

Likewise, people have grown so accustomed to having their dogs in the mix of all activities that it is fair to say that in most pet homes, *Canis familiaris* has reached the status of full family membership and is therefore subjected to all the rules of human interaction, often including holiday gifts!

Herein lies the root of so many problems that plague owner and dog relationships. Our pet assesses his relationship with family members from an animal-to-animal perspective and acts accordingly. As caring and empathetic beings, we oftentimes manage the relationship with our dogs as if they have been able to evolve human-like characteristics over the centuries, and we act accordingly, attributing human emotions and needs to our pets and often denying our dog's needs (for example, to follow the rules of the pack).

Given there are many parallels between rearing children and raising dogs, the critical point of divergence for those similar pursuits is the need for explanation (of duty and consequence). Even young children can appreciate commentary and carefully weigh in the balance a consideration for how future decisions will bring about certain outcomes.

But dogs, on the other hand, are animals of action. To manage them successfully, a handler must act, not confabulate. Our canine family member must experience the consequences of his deed in order to learn.

Many of the terms discussed in dog training correspond to the natural way dogs relate to one another such as *dominant, submissive, rank and order, alpha, territorial, pack,* and so on. The reason it's important as a dog owner to understand the dog's natural way of interacting is that from an evolutionary perspective, our canine family members are not that far removed from their wolfish predecessors. So things like who gets to eat what and who gets to lead the way and who gets to control what space and who gets to bully whom are all very important issues for dogs and in the dog's mind must be worked out as soon as possible.

We should not harbor ill feelings toward our canine companions for utilizing the tools afforded them from millennia of successful evolvement. We should keep in mind some of these tools like boldness and barking that we humans were directly instrumental in bringing about.

Yesterday at the training center, I worked with a five-pound Pomeranian and a one-hundred-and-ninety-pound English mastiff. Also yesterday, I handled a cocker spaniel so aggressive he had to wear a muzzle during training and followed this fellow with a collie mix so gentle that we carry out her instruction with a buckle collar and a whisper.

Because of this diversity in dogs and the unique nature of each home environment, I had to create a program that was not only effective for nearly any kind of combination but would be efficient, streamlined, methodical, and virtually foolproof. Within those parameters, I developed this ten-step approach to dog control.

I begin this book with the assumption that you already have a dog or dogs living with you as a part of your family. That is why you will not find in this book a chapter on how to select a perfect dog. I also assume that those who read this book will be working with dogs of all ages and breed types with endless variations of personality and working skill. In other words, I expect to encounter in my readership the very same diversity and challenges that I encounter every day at the training center.

With that said, use common sense when applying the general instructions in this book. No one knows your dog as well as you do! Visualize working through these ten training steps as climbing up a ten-rung ladder. Like a ladder climber, you cannot reach rung ten without stepping on rung nine first. Each rung is your support as you reach for the rung above it.

I suggest that you read the entire book before beginning actual hands-on training. Reading through all ten exercises will help develop the proper training mind-set and aid, I hope, in showing you where you are going.

At the training center, we feel that dogs are special animals, not human beings, uniquely designed over fifteen thousand years of selective breeding to accept and thrive in our families as their pack. Our dogs need to be handled with affectionate care and firmness, lest they retreat to their more basic animal tendencies—those that served their ancestors in the wild but are inappropriate as part of our family units.

Our dogs do best when we expect a lot from them and give them a lot in return. As owners, we have elected to take on the responsibility to humanely and safely harbor this special animal in the midst of human activity. As handlers, we should be positive, we should be firm, and we should be consistent. It goes without saying that we all love dogs, the writer and the readers. Our love of dogs is why we are joining up in this venture. I hope I can help you bring more balance to your own unique human-canine relationship.

My plan for this book was to create in print a series of private instruction sessions not much different from those you would experience in person at my training center. Countless times during this project, I felt as though I had bitten off more than I could chew in trying to guide a person I had never met through a relationship-building process with a dog I had never handled. But it is my hope that I have captured the essence of what I do every day in a format that makes it accessible to all family-dog owners.

As with any "do-it-yourself" instruction manual, the reader must be able to assimilate the general information that is being conveyed and then spin it to fit his or her specific situation. This is especially true in the case of dog training because each dog-handler relationship is unlike any other. This is why I stress again, read the entire book and develop as much of a dog trainer's mind-set as you can before beginning training. Absorb as much of our positive, consistent, firm philosophy as possible before trying to shape any canine behavior.

This is a basic training manual. All family dogs will be better family dogs for learning these lessons. However, some dogs have special needs. These are the dogs that may have been abused sometime before they were rescued. These are the dogs that may have been neglected. And frankly, these are also the many dogs who were just born to try your patience. I am currently working on a second volume which deals with more difficult problems in depth. If you are the owner of a special-needs dog, you will still need to train your dog through these ten steps first. It may be a bit slower, but I have never seen a dog in all my years who could not be trained.

Always remember too that dog training is neither perfect science nor flawless art. There is ample room for countless animal and human errors on the road to your new and improved relationship with your best four-legged friend.

I hope with the help of this book that you will be able to have your dog with you anywhere, anytime, and enjoy his or her company without a leash. In my nearly thirty years as a professional dog trainer, I have seen every kind of problem that dogs and owners could have together and I have developed over my lifetime of working with dogs a program that will work for almost every handler and dog. If you have a puppy, you are lucky. A lot of the early play I recommend with puppies leads naturally into obedience training. If you have an adult dog, whatever age, you are lucky. Your dog will have a longer attention span and will be more devoted to you. If you have a problem dog, you are in good company. Almost all dog owners wish their pets could make some behavior changes. And if you have a special needs dog that is becoming harder to deal with, this book is especially for you. Within this book are the beginnings of solutions to many of your problems.

I work at the training center with my two assistants, Dave Benson and Kathy Pruit. Every day, people bring their dogs to us for evaluation and obedience training. We rarely see a dog so rowdy or aggressive or shy that he cannot be shaped into an acceptable family pet with proper handling.

The crew (from left to right) Mathew, Kathy, and David

Some owners do not wish to train their dogs. They are afraid that training will make their dogs less spirited or that their dogs will like them less if they take charge of them. One woman came in with fresh wounds on her arm that her cocker spaniel had inflicted just that morning when she had tried to brush him. When we talked to her about training, she said she would rather her dog continue to bite her than to take a chance on crushing his spirit.

The woman with the cocker spaniel is an exception. She planned to keep her dog regardless of the weeping wounds. Many people who do not want to train their dogs eventually get rid of them (at the nearest shelter). In the United States a large percentage of the dogs taken to shelters are left there simply because they are not trained. At a certain point, dog owners have to wonder whether training is more disruptive to their dog than their pet's living in a shelter briefly until he or she is euthanized.

Trained dogs are, universally, happier dogs. Dogs live in a black-and-white world, and they are most comfortable when they know exactly what you, their owner and handler, expect of them. Dogs like the attention of training. They like the praise, and they like to achieve. Training your dog bonds you and your dog together in ways you might not have ever experienced.

I promise you that training your dog will not break his or her spirit. You will find that your playful Lab will still be playful and that your affectionate Newfoundland will continue to light up when you come into the room. Training only helps your dog find the self-control to make some choices that make everyone's life in your family, including his, more harmonious and happy.

Dogs are physical creatures that visually engage members of the pack, listen intently to activity in the distance, smell this, chew on that, dig for something else. Physical experience is the key to canine understanding!

What that means is that very little of the world comes to your dog in the form of verbal language. While your dog might know certain words and commands, your dog understands almost nothing of what you say to him. He can recognize a limited array of words, but mostly your dog depends on non-verbal cues to help him navigate in your family.

Our training method uses virtually no language at all, except praise, until we get to formal commands. We have found that dogs are often confused by their owners shouting, "NO!" and becoming agitated over unwanted behavior. The old-school notions of paddling with newspaper, rubbing your dog's nose in urine or feces while housebreaking, or shouting at your dog are not effective. These punishments seldom bring the good results the owner intends. Often, the dog fails to connect the punishment with the crime and becomes more confused or aggressive or shy.

Our philosophy in training is that to be successful in communicating with our dog, we must make the dog's world as black-and-white as possible. We as owners decide what behavior is acceptable and what is not in the context of our family. And once we have decided, we consistently insist on acceptable behavior. That is, if everyone in your family agrees that it is really cute that your dog jumps on you whenever he would like, then it is perfectly fine that your dog jumps. Your dog can do anything at all that *you want him to do* within reason. What a trained dog can no longer do is what you object to, however mild the objection.

Our program begins and ends in good manners. If your dog does not have good everyday manners, it scarcely matters that he can heel. Having good manners for us means that your dog will stop jumping on you and other people, he will stop mouthing you and others, he will stop begging for food, he will no longer bolt out the door nearly knocking you over, he will eat only what is offered to him, he will walk on your left side with slack in the leash, he will not approach visitors without an invitation, and he will stand still while you groom him. Only when your dog masters these skills do we begin the formal training with *heel, sit, down, stay,* and *come.*

Your dog, and whatever problems you have right now, can change. There is no dog that is too old to train and no puppy over sixteen weeks that is too young. You can improve your relationship with your dog in ten steps.

Equipment

The poor dog, in life the firmest friend
The first to welcome, foremost to defend.
  —Lord Byron, Inscription on the monument of his
  Newfoundland (1808*)*

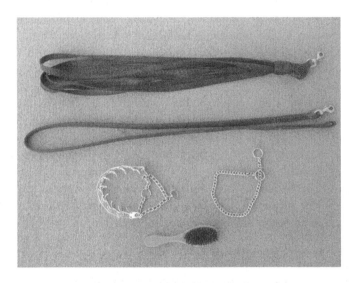

The bare bones of needed equipment

There are so many tools on the market for dog training these days, selecting what is right for your dog and his training can be a daunting task. Each tool was designed for a particular purpose: harnesses for pulling, buckle collars for restraining, muzzles for safety, and so on.

In order to accomplish all the tasks laid out in this book, you really only need a bare bones collection of tools: a training collar, a leash, a long line, and a crate. Any other equipment may be considered a plus but not absolutely necessary.

The Working (Training) Collar

Virtually all the dogs you see on television or in the movies, all the dogs you see competing at dog shows, are almost certainly trained with some fashion of working collar. For general control work or basic training, the slip collar usually works best because it emulates the natural way of disciplining for a dog. The quick grab and release of the collar resembles the corrective bite around the neck a subordinate would receive from a dominant member of the pack.

Therefore, when I refer to the dog's collar throughout any of the training exercises in this book, I specifically mean the slip (or pinch if necessary) type. The exception to this rule would be a pup younger than four months or any dog with a physical condition warranting the use of a buckle collar or harness. At the training center, we prefer the high-quality chain version over the nylon or leather slip models. The lightning-fast grab and release of the slip collar makes it most effective at redirecting a dog's focus, which is one of our primary concerns in obedience training. Anyone referring to this working collar by its misnomer "choke chain" probably doesn't know how to use it properly.

As a side note, for special cases (large powerful dogs, dogs with excessive drive or energy, and dogs with unusually high correction thresholds), a pinch training collar may be the tool of choice. The pinch collar works in a similar fashion to the slip models, except that it provides multiple grabs with each tug of the leash (pinch between each pair of links) rather than one. A new handler must keep in mind that the leash and collar action must be impressive enough to wean the dog away from the need of these tools altogether one day without giving up any of the genuine control that's been developed.

The Leash and Long Line

As far as leashes go for basic training, I recommend a sturdy four- to six-foot-long leather or nylon leash three-eighths to one inch wide, which should accommodate the size and strength of the dog in training while affording a comfortable grip for the handler. Although nylon is more resilient, leather (our choice at the training center) is more comfortable to handle.

Shy away from retractable leashes; they truly have no place in general control work. They are cumbersome to use and impossible to wean away from. Chain leashes also have a very limited purpose, and that's not for basic obedience training; they're very difficult to grip and usually too heavy for the task.

A long line is essentially a long leash in terms of dog training. For the purpose of this book, you will need a line at least twenty-five feet long but no longer than fifty feet. Nylon or polypropylene are the best materials for this tool because they are at the same time light and strong. When working a dog on a long line, we want him to have the feeling of the freedom of being off leash, while also affording the handler a secure hold.

What I prefer to use at the training center is a professionally made, ten-meter-long, three-eighths- to one-inch-wide nylon tracking line with a bolt snap at one end and a sewn-in handle at the other. You can use very effectively polypropylene rope purchased from a hardware store, cut to length and securely tied to your dog's working collar. As with the leashes, the width or diameter of the line (in other words, the total weight of what the dog is wearing) should be matched to the size and strength of the dog in training.

The Crate and Pen

Wire cages and plastic airline crates

Both you and your canine companion will greatly benefit from establishing a dog-secure area to utilize during training or anytime the home environment becomes hectic and you have no time to properly supervise your friend. This secure place should not be used for punishment or time-out. Think of it as a comfortable, private resting place where your dog is free from the intensity of interaction and the stress of making decisions. Most dogs appreciate the private space if it is used properly and will often retreat there on their own.

My choice for dog-secure confinement is the plastic airline crate (sold in most pet stores) for inside the house and a portable chain-link pen (usually sold in panels at building supply places) for the outside. A wire cage for the inside and a fenced yard for outside the house would be my second choices for suitable confinement. The actual dimensions of the crate or pen will depend on the size and requirements of your dog. In general, the size of the indoor crate should not be much larger than comfortable bed space (this will also serve as an invaluable tool for housebreaking), and the outside pen should allow for bed space, an elimination area, and a little pacing room.

10ft. by 10ft. portable chain-link pen

For my medium-sized German shepherd, I have a forty-inch-long by twenty-seven-inch-wide by thirty-inch-high plastic crate in the mud/laundry room. Outside, I have a ten-foot-long by ten-foot-wide by six-foot-high chain-link pen. I have this pen covered with a tarp that's secured to an A-frame roof system. This setup helps protect my dog against the hot sun and precipitation. He is quite comfortable in both, I might add, and eagerly runs into either one when directed.

Using the Equipment

Recollect that the Almighty, who gave the dog to be companion of our pleasures and our toils, hath invested him with a nature noble and incapable of deceit.
—Sir Walter Scott, The Talisman (1825)

Having the right equipment is not just important but necessary to dog training success. Before you attempt even the first of the handling manners, make certain all of your equipment is good to go, especially the essential training collar and the dependable leash. It almost seems silly to mention an equipment check before training except that I instruct people for a living and witness day in and day out the garbage used in an attempt to control the vast majority of dogs. Again, before you begin this program, get the equipment.

The backbone of our training program is to teach each dog to learn to build up and use self-control. We think it is essential to train a dog with a loose leash and the slip collar hanging open to simulate, as much as possible, the feeling of having no constraints. In every situation, then, the dog gets to make a choice about appropriate behavior. Example: Your dog sees a Pomeranian in her fenced yard from the road and longs to go to the fence and tell that Pomeranian a couple of things. You do not wish your dog to lunge over to the fence but to walk by your side. Your dog knows that he is on leash in the *walk* command and that *walk* means that he is not allowed to lunge in any direction, assuming you have accomplished the demands of the program through exercise 5. If the dog makes an inappropriate choice (lunges at the fence anyway), the collar very briefly bites the dog on his ruff (the best way to simulate a natural correction) where his mother and other dominant pack members would bite to correct. Your dog then remembers self-control and settles back to the *walk*. On the other hand, if your dog longs to go to the fence but chooses not to go and ignores the Pomeranian, he will at the very least get heartfelt praise from you and often a small treat. But in this program, your dog always gets the opportunity to make a choice and then gets the consequences of the choice: the quick bite of the collar or praise from you.

Slip Collar

We don't use your dog's buckle collar for training because the dog can feel the slight pressure of a closed buckle collar all the time, and there is no way for the collar to bite if and when necessary. But the slip collar, used appropriately, hangs open around the dog's neck 99 percent of the time in a training session. Therefore, even a dog new to training feels as though he's off leash 99 percent of the time he's being handled. The handler's competent application of this slipping device facilitates a much smoother transition to off-leash control (which is our ultimate goal) because the dog has experienced the freedom of loose-collar decisions and their consequences throughout the entirety of his training.

Do not attach your dog's tags to the training collar. Attach your dog's tags to the traditional buckle collar he will wear when he is not interacting with you. A sturdy buckle collar is also the choice equipment to anchor your dog by if that is ever necessary. Make sure the anchoring collar has a heavy enough buckle and is connected to withstand the force of your dog's weight and energy repeatedly hitting the end of the static line (assuming no shock spring is utilized).

The anchoring collar should also be wide enough not to eat into the dog's neck, allowing for periods of continuous pulling. It goes without saying, but I will say this anyway: **Under no circumstances anchor your dog with his slip collar.** In fact, it is a good idea to use the slip collar only when you or another family member is interacting with your dog.

(This opening discussion applies equally to the pinch collar which is, in essence, a magnified version of the slip chain collar. You can equate the pinch collar to a leverage tool utilized with large dogs and small handlers or tough dogs and soft handlers. In any case, try a slip collar first. Only if you find it necessary, consider the pinch collar. When buying and using the pinch collar, seek professional advice on fit and application.)

Here is the simple way to put the training collar on your dog. First, connect the leash or long line to one of the two rings on the collar. Second, hold the collar by the ring connected to the leash or long line snap in your right hand about chest high. Third, hold the bottom ring in your left hand so that as the right hand lowers, the links of the collar fall through this bottom ring creating a simulated noose. Fourth, hold both rings in one hand, keeping the noose open. **Fifth, reach out with your free hand to pet the dog on top of his head, and sliding your hand over his ears, firmly but non-aggressively, grab his cheek to hold his head while slipping the noose over his nose and behind his ears.** Finish by petting your dog, and relax!

When the collar is right side up (assuming the dog is on your left side) the run of the collar should pass from the snap of the leash through the floating ring over the top of the dog's neck. Even if the slip collar is put on upside down, it will still be effective

Putting on the slip collar

This leash and collar setup should be the only form of deterrent or negative consequences during all your dog handling, both casual and formal. In my method, there is no scolding, no anger, no negative emotion of any kind allowed from the handler during training. Dogs are physical animals. The best way to show them that they are doing something you don't want is by the correction of the collar, the bite, just as they would have learned in a pack.

I cannot overstate this: to train your dog quickly and successfully with the fewest false steps on the part of your dog, make sure the leash or long line and collar are in place prior to any interaction with the dog. I mean *any* interaction, not just training. Collar your dog up and let him drag his leash around before you play with him, before you hang out in the den together, or before the plumber comes in to look at the kitchen sink. This way, you will never be caught without the appropriate deterrent if your dog exhibits inappropriate behavior. Your complete consistency is necessary to your dog's quick success. If you are unable to properly supervise your dog, utilize the crate or safe area *before* your dog makes a bad decision.

To ease every dog owner's mind, I always follow this advice with the reminder that this learning condition is not permanent. If a handler is unfailing with this leash and collar application and is using the equipment the way I recommend, it is possible to wean away from it in a matter of weeks—months at the longest.

But do not worry about how long it will take to wean away from the training collar. You and your dog will get there. And every day will get easier, and every day, your dog will be a better dog.

Often my clients ask me why we must use a training collar. They have heard of dogs being trained by simply ignoring bad behavior and rewarding good behavior, or strictly baiting with treats to distract the dog from negative behavior.

First and foremost, I would say that a dog immediately understands and accepts the collar's pinching action as a negative consequence. In the wild, dogs are corrected by more dominant members of their pack by being bitten on the ruff of the neck. That is why when we talk about handling instruction, we refer to the collar correction as a bite. When you give your dog only positive reinforcement or treats, the message often confuses your dog. For instance, Aunt Mary walks through the front door to visit and your dog jumps all over the poor woman in a highly stimulated state of hysteria. Prepared for the moment, you offer your exuberant four-legged companion a treat as a bribe to stop mauling frail Aunt Mary. Unable to lure the dog's attention away from your now exhausted visitor, you employ physical restraint with a barrage of "No jumping" directives, finally bringing your canine friend to a halt. Immediately upon removal from Aunt Mary, you give the dog his just reward: a treat and "Good Boy!" So, in the dog's mind, what exactly is the handler positively reinforcing? Successfully mauling Aunt Mary maybe, or completely blowing off the "No jumping!" directive, or possibly allowing the handler to wrestle him to the floor. One thing is for certain, there are a number of interpretations from the dog's perspective as to what is most rewarding about that situation. (And I don't need to discuss how ineffectively positive reinforcement works when you call your dog and he doesn't come. The game is on and catch-me-if-you-can is so much more rewarding than anything the handler has to offer!)

Another reason for using a training collar is the minimized threat of the leash and collar action itself. Given that the correction is actually made by quickly pulling slack out of the leash and collar, the movement of the handler's body along with the force of the action itself is actually moving away from the dog, greatly reducing the dog's tendency toward defense. He experiences a bite on his neck, but the bite doesn't really seem to come from you. You are completely cheerful and calm.

A third reason the training collar is the most effective training tool is because it is the best, quickest communication device. If a dog owner understands that the training collar is a communication device and the dog cannot pull out of it, the owner will utilize the equipment much more efficiently and thereby utilize it less.

Here is how the collar works in training: During training, we give a dog the freedom of a loose leash and collar to allow for the dog to make a good decision. For example, you open the door and your dog generally bursts through it, nearly knocking you down. You want him to wait to be invited through the door. You open the door. As a handler, you need to be able to communicate to the dog in a timely fashion whether his behavior is acceptable or not. If the dog has chosen acceptable behavior (he looks up at you and waits for permission), we allow him the loose collar freedom to continue on, which is all the communication the dog needs to signal your approval. However, if the dog's course of action is unacceptable (he lunges through the door), we need to be timely with our disapproval. In this situation, it is hard to beat the slip collar action for timely effectiveness.

(I hate to belabor the point here, but if you choose a different method of training, shouting disapproval for example as your dog disappears, you will get nowhere with the training of your dog. He will be successfully out the door and having a gay old time going wherever he wants and returning when he feels like it. That is a great reward for lunging out the door. And if you are still mad when he returns, he might grovel a bit, but probably not. He got his reward: his gay old time in the neighborhood.)

Because the domestic dog is such an adaptable animal, he will eventually drop those *specific* behaviors to which these timely bites are attached and tenaciously hang on to those behaviors that bring about profit (praise and loose collar). The more timely a handler is in connecting a collar bite or loose-collar praise to a specific behavior, the clearer the communication becomes between handler and dog, resulting in less testing of rules on the dog's part and less reinforcing of the rules on the handler's part. This means, of course, weaning away from the leash and collar altogether one day.

I did want to mention one aspect of leash and slip collar training that shouldn't be overlooked: the ability of the handler (utilizing the equipment) to limit the dog's options of correction escape. Let's take, for example, your friendly, good-natured dog's overzealous interest in a visitor: the dog's tendency to jump on and mouth every visitor that comes through the front door of the house.

In this situation, we want to convey to the dog that he is not allowed to initiate physical contact. He must wait for the visitor to do so. We want to convey this idea without restraining the dog or muddying the waters with rigid formal commands like sit or stay. The presence of a visitor doesn't need to be a formal command exercise. In fact, using a command in this situation to keep the dog from making contact with the visitor or from running out the door may actually confuse the dog as to what we really want or why we corrected him. Ideally, we would like our trained dog to have the freedom to mingle with our guests without being obnoxious.

In order to communicate this clearly to our dog, we need to give him the loose collar freedom to choose his course of action. And we, the handlers, not the visitors, attach the appropriate consequences to his behavior. This is the point where the leash and collar are indispensable because we can supply a deterrent at exactly the right moment regardless of how agile the dog may be around the visitor or visitors. We can also prevent the dog from bolting out the door or running away from the challenge altogether. The dog needs to learn to shape his behavior (in this case, wait politely for the visitor's attention) to avoid correction and gain profit while in the presence of temptations (visitors).

This training is extremely hard to bring about without some sort of leash and training collar.

At the training center, we are frequently asked to give our opinion of the remote control collar as an alternative to the standard leash and slip collar.

I do believe that electronic collars have a place in dog training, a very specific place to be more exact. They are invaluable for training at great distances, for example, the training of hunting dogs during pointing, retrieving, and holding-at-bay exercises. Remote control collars can be the perfect tool for fine-tuning a high-level competition dog. We've worked with handicapped handlers at the training center who would have no chance of controlling their dogs without electric collars.

But what these high-tech collars are not is a shortcut to a finished dog. In virtually all cases, the basic leash and collar work should be done before utilizing one of these devices. And even then, I think that electronic collars should be used only by experienced handlers or under the supervision of capable trainers.

In my twenty-seven years of training dogs, I have found that there is no shortcut to achieving a sound, obedient relationship with your dog. You must clearly define the dog's role in your relationship with him or her by establishing rules and vocabulary that are consistent and reinforced with timely incentives and deterrents over an extended period of time. Although remote control devices can be useful in certain advanced aspects of dog training, there is no substitute for a standard leash, a training collar, and a consistent, cheerful owner.

I might mention here that on a regular basis, we have dogs brought into the training center wearing head halters. In most of these cases, the dog's owner is looking for a passive alternative to the training collar. The theory behind the device is sound; if you're strong enough to control the dog's head, you're strong enough to control the dog.

This theory and the devices that come out of this theory have proven to be immensely successful with horses for centuries. However, the head halter is meant to control your dog by physical constraint. **Since the animal never needs to develop self-control while wearing a head halter, the dog will not actually ever be trained to make decisions that are counter to his hardwired urges.** If you take the head halter off the dog, the dog resorts to the same behaviors as before. Therefore, for our purposes here, a head halter will never shape your dog's behavior independent of the halter. Unless your dog has some problematic condition with his neck, stick to the standard slip collar and six-foot leash for your dog's instruction.

Loose Leash

When should a handler acquire a leash? The answer should be *before he acquires a dog*, not sometime afterwards. A leash is an interactive device and a teaching tool. A leash is not a restraining device or a steering tool.

If your dog is older than three months, he should wear the leash attached to a collar anytime you interact with him (a buckle collar with pups younger than four months or any dog with a physical condition warranting such a collar).

Think of a dog wearing a leash during interactions as you would a man wearing a tie during work. Let's consider a young man fresh out of college. This young fellow has donned a tie a grand total of three times in his whole life: two graduations and a wedding. So when he launches into a new career with a company requiring ties as a part of their dress code, he'll have some adjusting to do. I'm quite sure that for the first weeks, there will hardly be a moment when the new employee doesn't feel that unwanted tie around his neck. I am also sure the tie will be awkward and in the way a lot during work, but that is just at first. Eventually, our new career man will adjust. The feeling of the tie around his neck will fade. It will seldom be in the way anymore. In fact, after a while, he might forget to take it off after he gets home. And after a longer while, the young executive might think of the tie as a symbol for success itself and take pride in wearing one.

So it is with a dog and his leash. If it gets caught under the door, un-catch it. If it gets wrapped around a tree, unwrap it. **As long as you're supervising the dog, he is in little danger of getting hurt.** Whether it's in your hand, underfoot, over his back, or dragging between his legs, your dog will get used to wearing the leash. All dogs do.

The leash is neither good nor bad, just necessary. You might even refer to it as his tail on the front end. He goes nowhere without it. As the awareness of the leash begins to fade in the dog's mind (as the tie did in the man's mind) what you and your dog gain in behavior-shaping with the leash attached will be mostly preserved during off-leash reinforcement. All would agree that the end goal for all dog owners involved in training is off-leash control. I think a person would be hard-pressed to find a better way to get there than by following these steps.

Having the leash attached to the dog (not necessarily in hand) during any kind of interaction means a positive solution to an unexpected problem is within reach. Since dogs, like people, are not 100 percent predictable, a handler should prepare for these unexpected challenges by always abiding by this rule until formal off-leash control is acquired—no matter how long this takes. By all means, hope for the best in any situation, but only the naïve fail to prepare for the worst.

All too often, we hear at the training center, "I didn't have the leash on him because we were *just* playing ball." That's when the dog decided to take charge of the situation and turn this game into catch-me-if-you-can-I'm-not-ready-to-quit-yet.

"He didn't have the leash on because I was *just* brushing him," a client says, seeming not to understand that her dog took charge of the situation and turned grooming into a wrestling match.

"He wasn't wearing the leash because we were *just* hanging out when my Aunt Mary popped through the door for a surprise visit, and Jackson mauled her with attention."

Remember there is no *just* anything if you truly want to gain off-leash control. Establish the pattern of behavior you prefer by always being prepared. If your dog is out of his secure area, the leash is on. Be generous with his rewards, but be ever ready with deterrents.

Be vigilant while your friend drags his leash about, because those canine molars can make short work of even the toughest leash. Remember, it's your leash and not the dog's. If you catch him licking or chewing on it, quickly and quietly grab the leash and snap it right out of his mouth. No apologies or comments are necessary.

For medium-sized dogs down to the toy breeds, the training leash needs to reduce in width and weight, but not in length, down to the light quarter-inch-wide products suitable for the smallest dogs.

We haven't found much use for the retractable models during training, although I understand their appeal, allowing more freedom for the dog. Our feeling at the training center is that we eventually reach much greater freedom for the dog by allowing for no leash at all when he is trained. Besides, retractable leashes tend to promote pulling and running amuck, two ideas we're desperately trying to get away from, not to mention that they are cumbersome for most handlers to deal with.

There is no real training without the loose-leash approach. Your dog must have the freedom to make decisions in every training situation. Whether you're talking about visitor control or dumbbell retrieval, a handler must set up free choice for the dog, followed by the appropriate consequence. Without this sequence, no genuine learning takes place.

At the training center, we insist on a loose leash or a long line through every step of training, starting with the very first moment of the very first instruction session. This is, beyond any shadow of a doubt, the most difficult directive for our new handlers to follow.

Affording the dog the freedom to choose his course of action sets in motion for the dog the process of association between behavior and consequence (profit or loss). Assuming that the ever-ready handler is completely focused on his canine pupil, he can quickly supply a sharp snap using his loose leash at the precise moment his dog commits an undesirable act. Likewise, the handler should be ready to reward the dog with the standard incentives (verbal praise, soothing strokes, or a treat) as soon as he sees behavior move in a desirable direction.

In essence, once a behavior has been thoroughly forged using a loose leash, off-leash response—which is our goal—is not far away.

Maintaining the loose-leash technique throughout training will only be difficult if a new handler temporarily loses confidence or concentration during an exercise (usually because of environmental distractions). We find that this loss of focus with new handlers is very common. And consequently, as instructors, we continually remind our students to loosen their leashes. As you work with your dog, concentrate to be sure the leash is completely loose except for a negative correction.

Dog-Secure Area

What should you do with your dog when you are unable to properly supervise him? Put him in a comfortable, secure area.

When I conduct a seminar for Babies "R" Us or a high school health-and-safely class or any other group of interested dog owners for that matter, early on, I present a list of do's and don'ts. One of the very first things I suggest that owners of untrained dogs do is set up a comfortable secure area for their four-legged family member. The secure area should be somewhere convenient and out of the weather. That could be an air crate in the laundry room or a portable pen inside the garage. You might designate an entire room in the house for this purpose or fence in the complete yard as long as you give the dog adequate shelter from the elements.

This is a good time to relay to you a curious experience I have each month. On the third Thursday of every month, I conduct a pet safety seminar for the Babies R Us store chain. There will usually be eight to twelve expecting couples attending. At some point in the seminar, I'll ask for a show of hands in response to a series of questions. The questions will run like this: "How many of you already have your nurseries ready?" Almost all hands go up. "How many of you have cribs ready to go for the new babies?" Almost all hands again. "How many of you here have substantial gear like car seats, playpens, infant seats?" All hands go up. "How many of you have dogs?" All hands go up. "How many of you have crates for your dogs?" Only two hands go up. "How many of you have dog-safe areas set up outside like a fenced yard or pen?" Maybe two hands go up. "Well, how many of you have training gear like slip collars, sturdy leashes, and long lines?" One hand.

I always ask the group, "Does this not shock you as much as it does me? You have all the substantial gear to secure, control, and rear the delicate human being who will be living in your home, and little or nothing at all to secure, control, and raise the powerful animal that already lives there!" Then we all laugh. But you have to agree it's peculiar.

Though I recommend using a crate, there are other ways to keep your dog safe. Your choice of confinement is limited only by a few conditions. First, the area must be escape-proof regardless of a dog's determination to chew, dig, or climb out (remember, you are dealing with a tough animal, not a soft human being). Secondly, no man or beast should be able to enter the area without the handler's providing access. Lastly, there should be nothing in your dog's safe area that would be wrong for him to have contact with.

I should also add that the crate is an invaluable asset when traveling, providing the dog with a familiar, comfortable place away from home and a margin of safety if you are unfortunately involved in an accident.

If a dog's confinement area is utilized properly for secure, comfortable quarters and never for punishment or time-out, it's a rare dog that will not grow to relish his own space, safe from disturbance.

Introduce your dog to his areas in the same positive praise and food motivated manner you introduce him to every new idea. Use a leash and collar if necessary; be interactive with the dog in the confinement area during the introduction process. As always, remember to be as determined as you are positive.

Shaping New Behavior:
A Brief Discussion of Current Ideas about Correction, Praise, and Release

The one absolutely unselfish friend that man can have in this selfish world, the one that never deserts him, the one that never proves ungrateful or treacherous, is his dog. When all other friends desert, he remains.
— George Graham Vest, Speech in Senate (1884)

Correction

No dog owner wants to, but every dog owner must at some point correct his dog because of unwanted behavior. I don't think anyone would disagree with the previous statement; however, many a heated debate centers on the question of how to deter unwanted behavior. How do you effectively and humanely correct a dog?

Should a dog owner actually punish or only withhold reward in the face of an unwanted canine behavior? Are verbal reprimands useful? Should a handler display negative emotion to show his dog that a particular behavior is undesirable?

I will be the first to admit that there are multiple answers for each one of these questions. What I can offer you here are answers to these complex questions derived from my nearly thirty years of work with more than ten thousand family dogs. My approach to handling any given inappropriate canine behavior will not be the only solution you will hear or read about for that particular problem, but I will give you what we at the training center have found works best for us.

There is no substitute for physical action from the handler when it comes to correcting a dog if you want long-lasting results.

Efficient, effective action is what every handler should be looking for. That is why we preach at the training center that you avoid corrective measures, even though they might be physical, that can bring about more negative behavior than you were dealing with before. For instance, rapping a feisty, back-talking pup on his nose or chastising him with a pointed finger will nearly always result in a more serious protest. Another common example of improper physical correction is paddling with a rolled-up magazine (or the like) for garbage can raiding or eliminating in the house.

This old-style discipline that involves the handler physically attacking the dog generally brings about an extreme reaction from most dogs—anything from aggressively lashing out at the attacker to submissive urination and hiding. Shouting, along with emotional explosions directed toward your companion, can wreak havoc on a dog-handler relationship, creating in the dog a distrust and uneasiness over a handler's volatility.

Other handlers suggest that the dog be given isolation for rule infractions. My feeling about "time-out" as a disciplinary technique is that it barely works for children. And children have the cognitive ability to connect how an undesirable behavior in the past prevents participation in the present. Since dogs exist in the moment and, at best, would have great difficulty making that obscure connection, leave out the time-out.

Withholding reward until the dog cooperates with the handler's permission is definitely a form of motivation. In regards to this technique as an effective training approach, however, there are a few complications to consider.

First of all, I would have to say that seldom is the training environment for the average family dog sterile enough (devoid of interesting distractions) to facilitate the dog's unbroken focus on the reward. It is much easier for our canine companions in most cases to find more easily attained pleasure than the focus the trainer is demanding.

This training technique of withholding reward also demands of the trainer intense concentration on nothing but the one dog and his single task (a level of concentration, I might add here, most new handlers have yet to develop) so that the handler can instantly recognize and reward his dog for any micro-movement in the direction of completing the task. This training approach requires many connected baby steps in the right direction in order for the dog to perceive the desired leap.

Above all, this withholding the reward strategy requires lots and lots and lots of practice on behalf of the trainer and lots and lots of time to shape canine behavior.

I have a good friend who is truly a connoisseur of competitive training, and he's been very successful utilizing this method of training on both rottweilers and German shepherds. Kevin is the embodiment of the patience and concentration needed to be effective with this technique all the way up to the competition levels. But even Kevin uses leashes and training collars to finish out and proof his dogs' responses around distractions.

So what is the efficient, effective action we find so desirable at the training center?

Nonemotional training collar action is the answer!

The types of training collar and the intensity of its use should be adjusted to fit the particular dog and the particular situation at hand.

There are some constants among the variables, however. **Minimize or eliminate altogether your negative emotions when administering the correction.** Make sure as the handler you do not direct your energy or the action of the correction toward the dog in an attacking fashion. Be calm and steady with your movements whenever possible.

Correcting for inappropriate greeting

Remember, we want the dog to connect the undesirable behavior with the unpleasant consequences. Try not to be an overwhelming presence because there is too much negative fallout between the dog and the handler if the act of disciplining becomes too personal. At the training center, we try to be mechanical with our corrections and personal with our praise, because the perfect balance for sharp, impersonal discipline is genuine emotional praise. Dogs definitely respond best to this combination. I would attribute the success of our training programs (a great deal of behavior shaping in a short period of time) to this one principle.

Up to about 1995, it was customary for me to encourage handlers to utilize a verbal reprimand in conjunction with a leash and collar correction the way we did as professionals at the training center. I thought a verbal reprimand added to the likelihood of success as long as the emphasis was placed on the physical part of the discipline. I knew even then that the physical action was the most important part of the experience for the dog (being the physical animal that he is).

Around that time, simply out of frustration that many of my novice handlers were making little progress with their dog's training, I began forbidding my clients from using reprimands along with their leash and collar when disciplining their dogs. My intention was to direct all their energy down the leash. I wanted to facilitate a more effective, efficient correction in hopes of eliminating unwanted behavior.

Before I imposed this moratorium on verbal reprimands, the average handler would aim 50 percent of his effort through the words *no, stop,* or *quit* or some variation, and only 50 percent of the handler's energy would make it into the leash and training collar.

As a result of the handler's tendency to verbalize instead of intensely correct, in many cases, the dog did not experience the negative consequence as being negative enough to eliminate the unwanted behavior. Consequently, I wound up with a substantial number of frustrated handlers and confused dogs unable to further develop their obedience relationship. And along the way, mostly due to the frustration of ineffectiveness, these handlers became more and more emotional with their discipline.

Now with the verbal outlet omitted, we have all but eliminated this type of correction frustration. For when handlers are forced to focus all their energy down the leash and collar, we have little trouble quashing an unwanted canine behavior because the negative consequences connected to that behavior are negative enough for the dog to avoid repeating it—not so with the reprimand and emotional outburst from the handler.

Also, with effective leash and collar discipline, we have much less collateral damage usually linked to loud emotional reprimands like submissive urination, aggressive protests, and hiding. I think two of the biggest pluses of all that arise out of this emotion-free, reprimand-free style of correction are the dog's speedy emotional recovery from the negative experience and his readiness to move on.

We found this tactic so effective with our clientele that we have followed this same approach ourselves, as professionals, and ever since have had the same successful results. The all-important variable in appropriate discipline or praise is the amount of it.

How intensely and how frequently should praise/discipline be given?

This delicate variable must be adjusted to fit the particular dog in training and the specific situation the handler and dog find themselves in. The more adept the handler is at adjusting the correction and praise to suit the dog and situation, the more successful the learning experience. Herein lies the challenge for all dog trainers, especially professionals who work with countless canine personalities in every imaginable situation with little time to fine-tune their relationship. Adjusting intensity and frequency on the fly is paramount to dog training success. Here are some guidelines:

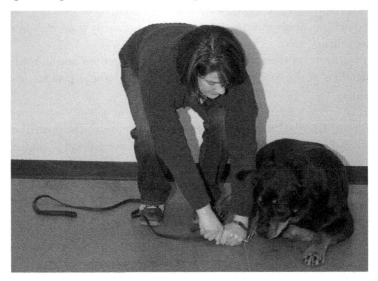

A diving style correction over a down

At the onset of any training, assume the dog you are handling is sensitive to corrections and has an inherently low pain threshold or is inclined to be submissive. Immediately prior to an exercise, before anything can go wrong, give your dog some good stuff like a treat, petting, and kind words. When the moment for discipline arises, quickly and stealthily snap the slack from the leash thereby causing the collar to grab the dog's neck. The slack should be as quickly returned to the leash as it was taken away, allowing the dog a loose collar and an opportunity to make another decision.

If this initial action was unsuccessful at curtailing an unwanted behavior or grabbing the dog's attention, repeat the leash snap and release immediately, using more force this time when pulling out the slack.

If you are still unsuccessful at changing your dog's mind, repeat this process using even more force and hand speed. Stick to your guns! Do not let up until you are successful at grabbing your dog's full attention.

Use your leash without speaking. Use your leash stealthily. We want to call as little attention to the equipment as possible. Our goal is to connect a negative consequence to an undesirable behavior with the dog perceiving very little of the leash, collar, or negative emotions of the handler.

If we are careful in connecting the behavior and consequences at this stage of on-leash training, we'll have little work to do when the dog graduates to off-leash training. Remember, by omitting reprimands and negative emotion, we accelerate the dog's emotional recovery from the negative experience and his readiness to move on to the next lesson. Demonstrate to your dog that the corrections you administer are not personal by genuinely praising him when he cooperates.

If you start off with light leash and collar corrections and immediately sharpen them as the dog or situation requires, it will not be possible to over-discipline.

After working with your dog a very little bit, you will develop a good feel for how much leash action is required to get his attention. Then you'll be able to skip the build-up process from too light to be effective and jump into the correction that works, minimizing the negative time along the way.

The right amount of correction (with no reprimand or negative emotion) reduces the stress load on the dog, especially if the handler remains positive and playful throughout the work (despite mistakes and discipline).

Try to move through the exercise as you had planned, even though the dog may require discipline to get through it. Keep moving through the exercise while you administer correction if at all possible. Do not stop and fight with your dog. If you do, the fight will quickly become the focus for both of you. Take charge of the immediate situation as proficiently as you can, remembering that the training collar action is an effective means to the desired end only if the action is negative enough for the dog to want to avoid it. Correction avoidance and positive incentives (physical patting, verbal praise, and food bonuses) are all the motivation your dog needs to cooperate.

Always keep in mind that the bite of the training collar action should be unpleasant but never physically damaging to the dog.

The last variable under this discipline heading we need to discuss is when. When exactly should you administer a correction to your dog when counteracting a negative behavior? When your dog thinks about misbehaving? When your dog commits to misbehave? (There is a clear difference between the previous two questions, and I will explain.) Or when your dog is deep in the midst of misbehaving?

The answer is that you should administer a correction when your dog commits to misbehavior: after he has made his choice between desirable or undesirable behavior but before he receives any profit from his undesirable choice. Determining the moment of commitment is not as difficult as most people make it out to be.

Let's look at a couple of examples. Imagine we're working with a rowdy, people-loving Labrador who loves to affectionately maul every visitor who comes through the front door. The undesirable behavior we want to get rid of is the rough physical contact the Lab initiates with visitors. Assuming we have set up the dog's learning experience as a training exercise, we have a helper as our visitor and the training collar with leash in place. This setup allows the handler to concentrate on just two things: the Lab's behavior and our goal not to allow the dog to initiate physical contact.

So when the observant, ever-ready handler detects even the slightest dog-initiated contact (paw on shoes, shoulder against knees, mouth on hand) regardless of how accidental or bold the contact appears, the handler responds instantly with sufficient correction to disengage the dog. In my opinion, it's wrong to allow this situation to escalate into a rough visit, which is guaranteed to happen in just a flash of a moment. Once this escalation begins, the Lab takes control of the visit and becomes nearly hysterical with stimulation, making regular corrections a cheap price to pay for such fun.

However, if we correct our Lab while he's considering rough contact but before he has committed to any, we might convey to him that the presence of visitors is bad news instead of the bad news being his visiting style. So we watch and wait until we see that slight movement toward dog-initiated contact.

With any training exercise, before any real dog work begins, the trainer must determine where *exactly* his line of unacceptable behavior lies. In doing so, the trainer knows the precise moment for precise action, whether it be a negative consequence for crossing the line or a positive consequence for stepping back from the line.

I would like to explore one more less obvious example of commitment to a negative behavior.

A common challenge we're faced with almost daily at the training center is eliminating the competitive issues between multiple dogs in the same household. One of the more volatile issues is the battle over food and treats, and that can be a bit tricky to deal with.

First things first: we must decide what the rules of food ownership are. Here are mine: For the dogs' regular meals, each dog has his own pan and station (the dogs being no more than a few feet apart). No dog is allowed to encroach upon another dog's feeding pan or station for any reason. When a dog is given a treat or bone, it is his exclusively until he walks away from it leaving all interest with the item. At that time, the treat or bone is free to any other dog. No dog is allowed to encroach upon another dog's enjoyment of his prize, period. No dog is allowed to pressure another dog into relinquishing his possession through posturing, threatening signals, or audible signals from *any* distance.

Now that we've laid out the rules, assuming leashes and collars are on, we hand out treats and focus on one thing: dog behavior. If I suspect that one of the dogs is contemplating breaking a rule, I do nothing but passively study more closely. When I detect the slightest movement, gesture, or sound that indicates to me, the handler, that one of the dogs is at this moment *barely* breaking one of the clearly defined rules, I step in for a leash and collar correction without delay.

If I am not quite sure that a dog is yet breaking a rule, I wait and watch until I am sure. The closer you study canine behavior, the easier it is to make the call. However, I prefer to err on the side of waiting too long for the correction rather than correcting too soon. Keep in mind that it is always okay to be a little late with discipline, but it is very destructive to be a little early.

Catching the dog at commitment is the key to successful correction. Give him the freedom to make his decision. That is how he learns. But don't allow him to gain too much satisfaction from his inappropriate decision.

Praise

The primary catalyst in building an obedience relationship is praise, not correction. Every dog owner's favorite part of training is doling out the good stuff. Mine too!

Labradoodles enjoying work

When I discuss praise here, I am speaking specifically of the positive consequences associated with the right effort. Talking to dogs is natural. Kind words calm our four-legged friends and make them feel comfortable and accepted, but this is different from praise. At the training center, we utilize three distinct types of praise: physical petting, audible pleasing words, and food as a bonus (never bait).

Unlike correction, which we administer in an impersonal or mechanical fashion, reward should be given with affection. There should be no mistake in your dog's mind about how pleased you are with his behavior. Approval should be personal.

The degree to which you express your pleasure or the amount of praise you dole out should depend on the individual dog being worked and specific situation at hand. For instance, an excited golden retriever may respond just right to a few kind words whereas a stoic chow may require some stimulating pats to elicit the appropriate response. Oftentimes, this same golden may find himself in the middle of a very demanding or stressful exercise and require a brief bit of stimulating play to lighten his load. And it would not be uncommon, working with a serious and mature chow, for him to need calming words to soothe and reward him as he follows his trainer through a difficult maneuver (for example, a large group of strangers).

Typically, when we reward a dog during training, we are after a certain level of response from our friend. This is definitely a delicate dance between too much stimulation and not enough reward. We don't want our dog in training to become so stimulated from our praise that she loses focus or forgets what effort she made to deserve this positive consequence. At the same time, we want to make her effort worthwhile and encourage more cooperation, because I assume that you, like me, are after a willing partner and happy worker.

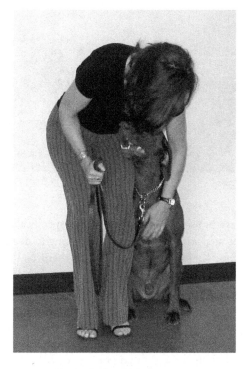

Rewards should be genuine.

In print, this aspect of a training relationship appears to be very natural, but if you were to hang out at the training center for a week, you would see that appropriate praising doesn't come all that naturally to most dog owners at first. As handling instructors at the center, we spend an inordinate amount of time coaching people on their praising style and timing.

Much of the time, we find that poor rewarding techniques create more of a disruption in training than they add incentive for effort. The easiest way we have found to rectify this situation is to dramatically slow the handler and the training process down. With the exercises literally moving in slow motion, the handler is now able to precisely touch or talk to the dog in a manner he thinks will bring around the proper response. And because dog and handler are moving slowly through this dance, evaluating the actual response elicited and making the necessary adjustments is very doable.

There really is a difference between a vigorous pat on the ribs and a heavy, slow stroke down the dog's head and neck. There really is a time and place for a delicately whispered, "That's my boy," but sometimes your dog really needs to hear a boisterous "Great job!" with some hand clapping. An observer doesn't even have to watch closely to see a markedly different response from the dog when these variables are adjusted.

Remember, too much stimulation from the praise and your four-legged pupil loses control and then loses focus so there is nothing gained. Too little stimulation from the reward and your four-legged pupil loses interest and then loses focus so there's nothing gained. If you move through the training exercises slowly at first, there will be no danger of falling into either of these traps. And praise can be for you what it is for us: the primary catalyst in building the obedience relationship.

Timing is as important in the application of praise during obedience training as it is with correction. If we want to ensure our dog will be crisp in response and as positive as possible, we must precisely connect the positive consequences to the dog's completed effort. It is important to get the praise in before there is a chance for a bungle. This is much easier said than done when you're dealing with a lightning fast Jack Russell terrier or a boxer bent on defiance and insisting on his own autonomy. However, we need to leave no doubt in the dog's mind that he received approval for a particular correct response.

Now let's talk about sweetening the pie! And for a dog, there is nothing sweeter than food. The right kind of food in the right amount at the right time can be the perfect motivator.

During obedience training or behavior shaping, food is best used as a bonus rather than as bait. The difference is that, with the food as bait, the dog's focus is on the food and not on the command, signal, or appropriate behavior, where it should be. When used as bait, the food is always visible and quickly becomes necessary in bringing about the connected behavior making it very difficult to wean your dog away from food as a consequence. When food is used as a bonus, however, food is nothing more than supplementary praise. Therefore the handler's command or signal and the dog's appropriate response remain the focus. When used as a bonus, food is not visible at all until delivery. The food then becomes essentially a dispensable item in bringing about desirable behavior and easy to omit altogether if a trainer wishes.

A little bit of food goes a long way.

When you work with food bonuses all day long as we do at the training center, you tend to get very particular about what works and what disrupts. The ideal food bonus should be tasty (to the dog) of course. Sometimes, this means a handler must experiment to find the perfect taste for a particular palate. I personally feel that any food product is a possibility as long as it is not harmful to the dog and falls within the following criteria: small enough for the dog to consume quickly, even on the move (pea to marble size); soft enough you don't have to allow time for crunching, crumb scrounging, and choking; manageable for the handler so it can be quickly grabbed and quickly released (not peanut butter or candy in wrappers).

A professional trainer who uses food as a reward will typically wear some sort of pouch on the small of the back or right hip. This way, the food is *easily accessible*, yet out of the dog's clear view. Keep in mind that if you want the dog to associate the bonus with a specific effort, quick, smooth delivery of the food is crucial.

If a handler clumsily manages the food, the intended bonus becomes too much of a disruption in concentration for both dog and handler and should be limited to the very beginning and the very end of a training period.

The amount of food bonus used during training is obviously up to the handler. I would suggest, however, varying that amount from one training session to another in order to further reduce a dog's dependency on food when working. I would add that at the training center, we are always very generous with our bonuses during stressful exercises. A food-wielding trainer should also factor the bonus calories into the dog's total daily diet.

Release

How do you tell a dog he is all finished with an exercise or responsibility? The best approach is to develop a unique command or signal for this one purpose only. The signal can be anything from a verbal "all done" to snapping your fingers, as long as you don't use that signal for anything else.

I begin by developing the release signal as soon as I start teaching my dog his formal commands. In fact, a trainer can't properly teach or reinforce a command without developing a release right along with it, because with the release command, we introduce at the onset of training the all-important tenet that the dog cannot adjust the rules set up by the handler. If we let our new pupil release himself even by accident, he quickly learns the formal rules like *heel, sit, down, stay,* and *come* apply only until something strikes him as more interesting. That would mean that no command taught to the dog would have any power to control his drives, desires, or energies. At best then, the handler's control would be tenuous and ephemeral rather than secure and dependable, as it must be in order to have value of any kind.

It doesn't hurt in the pre-formal-training days to set up an association between your release signal and treats or praise or play. A handler can begin this preconditioning at any age and establish a positive connotation with the signal early on. Keep in mind, however, that as formal training with specific directives begins to take shape, the release signal should be molded into an "at ease" cue rather than a "go wild" cue. The intensity of or the freedom allowed by the release can be adjusted by the amount of touch, food, or emotion coming from the handler.

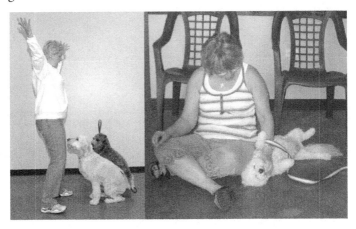

Both handler and dog should enjoy working.

Remember that release signals bring relief from the stress and responsibility for the dog and should be used frequently throughout rigid training. (However, when teaching composure and manners, there is never a release for the dog. These are behaviors you expect at all times.) At the training center, we usually run through a series of commands or exercises before releasing a dog. But in some circumstances (like a *down* command with a very dominant dog), a release signal is called for after a brief response to a single command.

Keep in mind that the release doesn't mean that the dog is allowed to fall back into any of the behaviors you have deemed to be undesirable while developing the handling manners with your dog. For example, there is never to be any running in the house.

The Handling Manners

Near this spot are deposited the remains of one who possessed beauty without vanity, strength without insolence, courage without ferocity, and all the virtues of Man without his vices. This praise, which would be unmeaning flattery if inscribed over human ashes, is but a just tribute to Boatswain, a dog.
—Lord Byron, Inscription on the monument of a
Newfoundland dog (1808)

Training your dog does not take great blocks of time. It is much more important to work frequently with your dog than to work for long periods. I suggest fifteen- to thirty-minute instruction sessions a couple of times a day as optimal for novice handlers and untrained dogs. That's plenty of time to accomplish big things without handler or dog lagging too severely in concentration.

When talking to clients, I compare these ten training steps to ten rungs on a ladder. When I was a kid, my uncle had a ladder with the third rung missing. That ladder was almost impossible to use. We would always try to turn the ladder so that the missing rung was close to the top where we might not need to go.

These ten steps are like the rungs. The skills build on each other. You cannot skip over one to get to another and hope to make the fastest progress toward getting your dog free of a leash all together. The first five rungs on the ladder, the five manners exercises, are the foundation for general control or pet obedience. They can be looked at as the core of your new, balanced relationship with your dog. At the training center, we begin all basic obedience and problem behavior solving with these handling manners and we finish by emphasizing their importance in order to maintain control over any dog long term. Realize that obedience training is a relationship-building process centered around three concepts or responsibilities for the dog: energy and drive control, handler deference, and distraction management.

Exercise One: Composure and Grooming

Composure

Remember that we are always teaching the dog self-control. We want him to control his natural, survival impulses and respect you as the alpha presence in his environment. These beginning exercises are informal. We want to be anything but an intimidating handler towering over the pupil during this composure exercise.

To teach the dog to find composure and, later, to accept grooming calmly, the handler should begin this lesson seated on a sturdy but utilitarian chair like the plastic patio kind. **The seated posture (for the handler) is important here because we need the dog not to perceive the owner as an ominous, towering threat, but a more informal presence.** We want to control the dog without the formality of commands and give him freedom within limits. Teaching the handler and the dog to hang out together without using rigid formal directives is the all-important design of beginning training, and it is a significant difference between our instruction program and the rest.

Hanging out with ease

With the handler seated, the leash and collar on the dog, and the leash in the handler's hand, allow the dog about two feet of loose leash. Your dog should be allowed to sit, stand, lie down, pace, adjust, sleep, roll over, levitate, stand on his head, anything so long as the two feet of leash remains absolutely slack and the dog does not bother the handler or anyone else in any way. And by that, I do mean *no* bothering in *any* way.

It is perfectly fine for handlers to pet and talk to their dogs freely (but never constantly) as long as the dog has not coerced or bothered his controller into this reaction. The use of food for a periodic bonus (attached to desired behavior) can be very helpful in bringing about sustained calm focus on the handler during this lesson.

The challenge here is not to entertain or restrain the dog, but direct the dog into self-control and composure by correcting the dog for undesirable behaviors like straining against the leash, chewing on the leash, crawling under chairs (no hiding from responsibility), or nosing head under arms and legs to bring about petting or wrestling. We also work to keep in check behaviors like pawing, mouthing, barking, and whining at the handlers or others. At the same time, a good handler is looking to seize every opportunity to hand out reward for effort in the right direction like brief moments of calm, interest pulled away from a distraction (that's none of his business), a withdrawn foot (that was about to paw), settling to a down at your feet (rather than crawling under the chair), choosing a passive sit (waiting for your attention) rather than jumping up into your lap demanding attention, and licking rather than mouthing.

Hanging out from the very beginning

Encourage normal activity in and around the training environment while your composure instruction is going on to condition the dog to what is natural, but use common sense and don't overload your friend with temptations in the early days of instruction.

Keep in mind during this exercise that the handler is a consequence supplier, not a hitching post. When you handle the situation this way, the dog is compelled to develop his own self-control mechanisms, whatever they might be. We are actually training the dog to deal with boredom. That's why we suggest no chew bones or toys be available for the dog during this particular lesson.

As soon as possible, drop the entire leash on the floor to demonstrate to your buddy that the leash in hand is not necessary to deter bad behavior. Be ever ready to grab the leash and use it when called for, but then drop it again to dare your buddy to take advantage of the relaxed situation. My feeling is that if we get this testing out of the dog's system early in training, it won't be necessary later when the training phase is over.

Remember, passive interest toward people, animals, or activities is perfectly all right. Even climbing up in the handler's lap is okay, as long as an invitation comes first. A handler should be careful to avoid too much lap time, for often, this turns into mollifying or pacifying, and the goal of self-control will not be achieved.

When you are watching television with your family, when you are eating dinner, when you are reading the newspaper—whatever you do—be sure that your dog is wearing his slip collar and leash. It is important that you consistently reward and correct for the very same behavior every time, so be sure before you begin that you know what behavior is tolerable and what behavior is not. It might take as much as a week of patiently making sure that your dog is always composed when he is around you.

Grooming

At the training center, just as soon as we shape the dog into some semblance of composure, we begin grooming control. To us, these two ideas seem to be naturally connected, and since grooming is too important to put off very long and since it is a more interactive form of composure, we look at the dog's composure while being groomed as part of his general composure training.

Besides the leash, collar, and chair, the only other tool a handler needs to develop grooming control is a simple wooden- or plastic-handled bristle brush. This brush will serve as a training substitute for all the real grooming tools which will be utilized later, such as nail clippers and irrigation bottles.

We set up this lesson with the dog broadside, directly in front of the seated handler. In this early stage of training, it's not necessary to insist on a stand or sit position for the dog. That can be developed later. What is important at this stage is the dog's cooperation, so he should not be allowed to squirm or wrestle or resist. The leash is typically held in the hand corresponding to the head end of the dog, allowing for a short but loose leash. With the brush in the opposite hand, the handler begins lightly and calmly brushing the dog along the withers and back. Remember to always monitor the dog's behavior because the focus of this exercise is not good grooming but behavior shaping. The goal the handler should be shooting for is calm acceptance by the dog of any grooming or caretaking, no matter how stimulating or repulsive the dog may find it.

Grooming should be easy, even with tough guys.

We start the brushing process at the shoulder because we have found after thousands of grooming sessions that this is the least sensitive spot on the dog and therefore the easiest brushing to tolerate. After all, we want this experience to be as pleasant as possible while we kindle a feeling of accomplishment in the dog. As always, the handler closely monitors his dog's behavior, looking for opportunities to reward his dog for any efforts toward acceptance or self-control. No doubt, along with these efforts, there will also be attempts by the dog to thwart the handler's manipulations, usually in the form of dancing, wrestling, chewing on the brush, or simply trying to get away. Correcting a dog for these undesirable behaviors can be especially difficult because a handler needs to push on through the grooming process while the checks are being made. The handler demonstrates to the dog that the exercise will not be altered or aborted, no matter how determined the dog is to influence the handler. If necessary, drop the brush and manage the leash with two hands in order to restore control. Then immediately pick up the brush and resume grooming. Don't forget to reward the dog at the first sign of cooperation and take frequent, very brief breaks following any kind of success during the grooming process.

As soon as the dog calmly accepts brushing over the easy area, gradually move on to more sensitive spots eventually covering the dog's entire body, including face, feet, belly, and tail.

Once brushing is under control, ear cleaning, teeth checking, and nail clipping should begin, keeping in mind we are only conditioning the dog for the real thing. That's why real nail clippers, ear cleaners, and toothbrushes are not needed at this stage of handling. In fact, the smooth wooden or plastic handle of the bristle brush will serve as all our pseudo grooming tools. After all, our only goal right now is to bring about calm acceptance in the dog for any manipulation we deem necessary such as isolating each toenail with one hand while the other hand presses the brush handle against it or raising the ear to explore the canal or raising the lips and opening the mouth to check the teeth, all along keeping the leash handy so that misbehavior can be dealt with swiftly.

Only pretend nail clipping in the beginning

Unlike simple composure work, the grooming sessions should be very brief in the beginning, no more than a few minutes at a time, because many dogs find this total self-control during grooming manipulation exhausting. And we do want this whole experience to be as positive as possible since it will be for the most part a lifelong endeavor. So lay on the praise and reward at every opportunity. Every day, when you are interacting with your dog, try to get a little further into grooming control. Be patient and quit before your dog tires and loses focus. Don't forget that your dog needs to be groomed on both sides and practice alternating sides.

Exercise Two: Food Control

Setup is just like for the composure and grooming exercise (seated handler, informal, loose two feet of leash, and no commands). Similar to the previous lessons, we begin with the easiest temptations: food. A helper comes in with lunch and sits immediately in front of the handler within the dog's reach, given the two feet of slack. When the helper sets the food on the ground (preferably within an open ziplock bag to provide a little added protection against the dog outmaneuvering the handler and getting a reward for his determination), the handler needs to be at the ready to quickly show the dog, with speedy leash corrections, that this food is off-limits. The helper needs to simulate the eating process (to enhance the dog's interest and to create realism) accidentally on purpose dropping parts of the lunch ever closer to the dog.

The handler rewards and corrects the dog in the usual fashion, showing him along the way the only food he gets is from the handler, regardless of how delicious and available the helper's lunch food may appear to a lip-licking hungry dog.

Throughout all of these temptations that are exercises in the dog's further development of self-control, the handler may notice trembling in his dog early on as he forms his rudimentary self-control mechanisms. This doesn't mean that your dog has now become afraid of grooming brushes, visitors, and food. It simply means that this self-control work is very difficult for him in the beginning. It will become easier with each lesson, and the trembling will subside. Eventually, all these exercises will be practiced hands off the leash, with the handler removed from the immediate work area, and they will present little or no challenge to the dog.

As a trained companion, your dog will be able to eat just *two things*: anything given to him by a primary handler or anything in *his* food bowl. Nothing else! This means, as a primary handler, you could share your French fries with your companion, but your sister shouldn't. Your dog could eat pizza from his food bowl but not from the coffee table. I tend to shy away from that kind of food myself, so I sure don't want to get my dog hooked on it. But my point is that it's not the type of food that makes it right or wrong; it's the way it's delivered.

Who is the primary handler, by the way? Any and all members of the dog's immediate family who are willing and able to forge an obedience relationship through consistent, regular training.

Place the food close to the dog, but do not offer it!

There are three critical ideas a dog owner must consider when working through this food-control exercise. First of all, preventing the dog from successfully stealing food is paramount in the development of self-control. That is why the use of open plastic bags that contain delicious temptations is so important. During a training session, if a dog happens to beat the handler to the punch and grab the bag containing a couple of bacon strips, there's ample time for the handler to take corrective action with the leash (forcing the bag to drop from our buddy's mouth) before even a morsel of bacon can be consumed. By this simple preparation of placing the food target in a bag before training begins, we help to ensure there will be no profit coming our dog's way for assertive behavior against our wishes.

The prevention of stealing when the dog is off the training clock is just as important a responsibility for the owner as effective handling during a session. This means for the dog absolutely no unsupervised time around food that is not his. Period. And we're talking about primary handler supervision, leash-and-collar-on supervision.

Try very hard not to work against yourself on this food-control issue. Don't leave food out on the counter or next to the counter's edge any longer than necessary. Don't assume your dog is sleeping soundly enough that when the cat is eating dinner in the same room, you can run upstairs and brush your teeth. Don't think your dog won't snatch a cookie from one of your small children if you turn your back for a split second.

These precautions against training failure are especially important in the early days of food control work because in this stage of relationship building, the dog wants to find out if there are any loopholes in the obedience contract. Your dog must test the new rules to make sure they are set in stone. Don't show your dog that you are unsure. As the days turn into weeks, your dog's testing and sneaky behavior will subside as long as he is not too successful in challenging the new rules during the process.

The second idea worth heavy consideration during this second obedience exercise is a realistic setup for the training environment as soon as possible. Move from the chair-and-helper setup to the kitchen (during dinner preparation), to the family room for pizza and a movie, and to the dining room with guests at the table (really eating) at the first opportunity. Have your training plan well thought out before the dog is allowed to enter the arena. Prepare several bags with food, inform your guests about the training procedure, and most important, make sure your dog is wearing his collar and leash before the training begins.

Be certain that a primary handler is designated prior to the dog's arriving on the scene because swift action is a must during this training procedure. See to it that a bag of temptation falls from the kitchen counter and the dining room table. Leave a piece of pizza (in a bag) on the edge of the coffee table during part of the movie. Allow your dog to move about freely (dragging his leash) and be ever ready to instantly check him with leash and collar action for any commitment whatsoever, audible or moving, toward one of the targets.

Be casual, be normal, but be observant.

Also, don't be in a hurry to pick up the bags. Constant exposure to food is part of a family dog's life. Only when the training session has concluded should you be sure to remove the dog from all temptations or remove all temptations from the dog.

The last critical idea of food control is commitment. Every handler must be observant enough and informed enough to recognize a dog's coveting behavior and then be willing to take action to effectively quash this undesirable behavior. For instance, the easy-to-recognize (albeit cute and often comical) begging behavior needs to be nixed if you ever hope to relax around your companion and food. Begging allows your dog to fixate on something that's not his and should be handled with a leash correction.

If you happen to have more than one dog in your house and one happens to be a fast eater, don't allow the fast eater to hover around or encroach upon the other dog's feeding station. I think it is a good idea to feed animals in the same area at the same time (leashes and collars on) to drive home the point that what is given to the first dog is not in any way for the second dog.

By the same token, your dog's hanging around for food to fall off a high chair, which quickly turns into a waiting game for your dog, is no good. If you want, after the little person has finished throwing things off his high perch, remove the chair from its original spot and give your dog a clear invitation to come in as the clean-up crew. Only when the primary handler gives the dog an invitation does the food become his.

I had a client not too many months ago with a very nice twelve-month-old Great Dane. Needless to say, this fellow possessed a voracious appetite and was notorious for stealing food off the table. After our first lesson, the client was so excited about her Dane's newfound self-control, she immediately went home and put the food exercise to the test. She called me the next day with a glowing report. "Charlie didn't touch a thing on the table. He just stood there with his head directly over the plate of chicken and didn't attempt to eat any of it."

I was happy she was so tickled, but all I could envision was this one-hundred-and-twenty-pound monster breathing and drooling on the chicken. So after praising her efforts, I instructed her to back off a bit to make the dining situation a little more comfortable for everyone. As a general guide, if you feel uncomfortable with your dog's coveting behavior, take decisive action right away. Don't wait for the bite out of the birthday cake!

A closing thought: I realize these self-control exercises are challenging for your dog. But you have to look at it as the cost for the privilege and comfort of being a family dog. And don't forget that the dogs I see coming to my training center live better than a substantial number of the world's population of human beings. Most of our dogs have better shelter, medical care, and diet than a lot of people, so a little responsibility is not a bad trade for all the benefits.

Any of the sections in this book that involve great detail in setup or exact handling technique should be reread and reread until the information seems clear and familiar.

Exercise Three: Visitor Control, Humans and Animals

Regardless of whether we're interacting with our dogs at home or away, there is one thing we can count on: We can influence the behavior of a visitor very little, but we can influence the behavior of our dog a great deal. So it is ultimately up to the trained dog to respect the rules of proper interaction. That is the way we see it at the training center anyway. Although the rules for proper visitor interaction are relatively simple (a dog is not allowed to initiate contact or force engagement), the rules can be difficult to teach.

The dog's role during a visit should be passive; the dog should wait to be interacted with. He should not be allowed to initiate physical contact regardless of what a visitor might say or do. If the dog is invited by the visitor and we approve of the visitor's invitation, we allow our dogs to reciprocate within the bounds of acceptable contact (no jumping, mouthing, pawing). We will not allow our dogs to force engagement by whining or barking at the visitor in an attempt to elicit interaction. It really does not matter how excitable a dog may be or how stimulating a visitor is. These rules are a must, and every dog that passes through our training center is taught to abide by them.

With these two rules in place, the visitor now has the option to interact with the dog or not, rather than having the dog shove the interaction down the visitor's throat. And ultimately, it's the handler calling all the shots as to who visits and how long, and that's as it should be. The guidelines we've just discussed are equally valuable when dealing with aggressive dogs. The only real difference is the type of contact or engagement an aggressive dog may commit to (a bite rather than a jump or a growl rather than a whine) and the seriousness with which the situation is handled.

We have found the easiest way to set up this training scenario is to begin with composure practice relatively close to an entryway or door into your training area. Setting up entry into the training area from behind a closed door is best. Have a friend or neighbor who will be your helper pose as a visitor. This "visitor" should knock or ring a bell before opening the door, creating the feeling of a real visit and bringing about a natural reaction in the dog which is generally at least a heightened sense of alertness.

Visitors should follow the handler's instructions.

This first visit should be looked at as a human-to-human visit. Our helper should ignore the dog in training. This will be the only style of visit until the dog can easily manage the human-to-human interaction. Then the helper can begin gradually directing attention toward the dog. By "easily manage," I mean the dog is command free, correction free, with the leash out of hand, hanging out while the humans visit. No commands should be necessary to control the dog. He is free to sit, stand, lie down, levitate, or in general just peacefully hang out for the duration of the visit.

When the pseudo-visitor enters the room, he or she should behave in a calm and natural way, approaching the handler and dog as a real visitor would. Keeping the visit low-key at first gives a dog that is new to this kind of training a better chance to grasp the rules and accept his responsibilities. And at the same time, a low-key visit gives a new handler a better chance to be timely with his rewards and deterrents, facilitating better learning for the dog.

As the dog's and the handler's proficiency rise, so should the intensity of the visit. The helper(s) should gradually portray wilder, louder, and more assertive visitors. Sometimes the handler allows the helper to make contact with the dog and sometimes not. **Remember the dog handler always controls the visit.** During a training exercise or in real life, no one interacts with your dog unless you say so.

It is very important to practice this exercise in different locations with different helpers. Sometimes the trainer is standing; sometimes you and your dog are walking in the park. The more realistic the lesson, the easier the control transfers to genuine visits.

Who is a visitor anyway? Any living being who is not a primary handler. Your young children, your Aunt Mary visiting for the holidays, the house cat, the delivery man, the dog walker and his dog—all these are visitors. This means that your four-legged friend's responsibility is to wait for physical contact from these guests in his domain. He cannot initiate contact.

This doesn't mean that he's not able to interact with others anymore. He simply needs to be patient, and he'll probably receive more positive attention from others since they're not busy defending themselves against his onslaught of affection and excitement.

Patience will bring about rewards.

Your canine friend will be free to respond to a visitor's contact by licking, rubbing, or smelling, but never with feet or teeth on their bodies. Not even when Uncle Charlie says, "These are old clothes. I invited him to jump on me," can your dog jump on Uncle Charlie. Unfortunately, neither Uncle Charlie nor your dog is boss. You are, and that means no jumping and no mouthing.

You could take time to explain to Uncle Charlie that if you make an exception to the rule for him, the dog is going to be much more likely to jump on frail Aunt Mary because the dog thought she invited him to jump up. Or you might tell Charlie the next time he comes over in nice clothes that the dog will not understand why he can't immediately jump on the man who enjoys it so much. Or you might just say that you don't want your companion to jump on anyone because he will always think there is a chance he might jump on someone and that thought or behavior will never fade away. Or you might just say nothing since you're the boss.

Now let's imagine the house cat comes running into the living room where the family and dog are relaxing. Most of our clients during their initial visit tell us that their dog and cat love to play with each other. But after a little bit of discussion, we determine that the cat rarely if ever initiates the contact or play. In fact, we find that in the majority of cases, play for the cat means nothing but escape or evade the much-too-rough and offensive contact the dog initiates.

What happens all too often is that the cat's peaceful home has been turned into the enemy camp where he must sneak around upon the dog's arrival. This can also be the situation for the very senior dog of the household when a younger, more spirited companion is brought in.

As soon as the visitor's rules are set up, peace and balance once again reign in the home because the cat or the frail senior dog are free to initiate contact with the dog in training, when and if they wish. And when the opportunity arises, the dog in training is allowed to reciprocate with appropriate behavior (not too rough).

When is a visit over? As soon as the visitor withdraws contact or engagement. It has nothing whatever to do with the dog's preferences. We want to make clear early on that this is no longer *The Molly* or *The Max Show*. This is at long last your very own show, run the way you like it!

This applies to my advice too. Remember that I work for you. Use this book as you wish. What I have essentially done here in this section, as in all the sections in this book, is lay out for you the reader the straight and narrow, the most direct path to real control. Deviate from this path all you like. Put your personal spin on any of these exercises and you can still end up with a balanced, orderly relationship with your dog. Keep one thing in mind, however: I am sure this way is the most dependable way to keep a happy, responsible dog. Should you decide to deviate, sometimes it gets more difficult to get and keep control.

Let's consider a few examples: Imagine you're walking your friend at the park when a familiar person approaches with her wild and friendly dog in the lead. There's nothing wrong with allowing your dog to instantly engage in wild, rough play with the visiting dog and end up jumping all over the familiar person at her invitation. Just keep in mind that this quickly becomes the norm for your dog, and he generalizes that this behavior is fine with you and is what you expect. It's simply a fact that the more your dog engages in unwanted behavior, the more he will want to do it! This unwanted behavior is his natural, instinctive behavior. And if this is okay with you, then it is not wrong. You're the boss.

But what I find is usually the case is that out-of-control behavior is not okay for the majority of dog owners. Most owners simply want to avoid the awkwardness of enforcing control in the presence of someone promoting the opposite.

I would be lying to you if I said I didn't feel somewhat self-conscious in that situation, controlling my dog and asking for a little help from the familiar dog walker. But I am fifty years old now and I have been handling situations like that all my adult life, so it really doesn't bother me as much as you would think. Besides, the proper upbringing of my dog, like my children, is way too important to me to worry about how someone feels in regard to my actions.

I remind you, the reader, that diligent, realistic training in and around the home environment will prepare you for those public encounters so that there is only a little behavior to work on under the scrutiny of uninformed eyes.

Can primary handlers afford to give their dogs special privileges during interactions with them and not affect good manners with visitors? Absolutely. I do. I invite my German shepherd to jump up on me, just so I can bear hug him. This privilege helps shed stress during demanding training, and besides, I like it. But I better not catch him jumping up on anyone else!

I also like to wrestle with my buddy, and there will be some mouthing allowed. (We both like to play rough.) Tug-of-war is one of our favorite games, but during all these activities, I am still in control because of the relationship I've built with him over months and years of training. When I say play is over, it's over. If, as a new handler, you have yet to develop this kind of authoritative relationship, your dog should not yet be allowed some of these privileges.

Regardless of the freedoms you allow your dog within your unique relationship, make sure you demonstrate to your companion in no uncertain terms that these freedoms do not carry over to non-primary handlers. I have never had a problem convincing any of my dogs throughout my life of this truth. And my dogs, being virtually cut from the same cloth as your dogs, have never shown any confusion or anxiety over this matter.

These kinds of freedoms or privileges can be allowed between family members and pets without fear of carryover to outsiders. Be determined and convince your dog through appropriate consequences that this is the way you want it. After all, it's your show.

To close out this section, I want to present a special concern in regard to deterrents during visits. Typically, when a dog is approached by a visitor (man or beast), excitement explodes within the dog in a very brief moment. As with any emotion that swells within the dog, including rage or fear, the more the emotion takes control of the dog, the less the handler can. The higher the emotion rises, the more intense the focus becomes on the target and the more closed the channels of communication become between the handler and the dog. And as the dog's emotional intensity rises, so does the dog's pain threshold.

So to take control of a dog during a visit scenario early on in training, a handler must be observant and at the ready with leash and collar action. If a handler can recognize the first micro moment of commitment to the visitor and seize that opportunity by supplying a modest leash snap or two (speedy removal and return to the slack leash), generally, a dog's focus will return to the handler and the excitement over the visitor will quickly wane.

As the dog's focus returns to the handler and self-control, be sure to lay on a good measure of reward (physical petting, verbal praise, or food reward). We want to demonstrate to the dog from the very first exercise that the approach of a visitor can mean good things like praise, reward, and even contact from the visitor if the dog can keep his self-control. If the dog chooses to take advantage of his loose-leash visitor opportunity and attempts to initiate contact or force engagement (by barking or whining at the visitor), the dog should only receive negative consequences (the necessary leash and collar tugs to redirect his focus and the absence of visitor contact and engagement).

Keep in mind that the handler in no way should restrain the dog to prevent contact or else the dog's manners will become the owner's responsibility for the rest of his companion's days. The main goal of this training program is to bring about leash-free control over our canine companions who are centered on self-control. Allow your dog to make decisions; you supply the consequences. Real leash-free control over your dog is truly that simple. Get your dog in the *habit* of doing things the right way, and that's all he will think of!

Keep in mind that there are no commands through this lesson and that the dog is always, except for corrections, on a loose leash. We're after self-control in the dog. As I say many times a day: He makes his choices, and you supply the corresponding consequences.

The dogs are free to make decisions; the handlers supply consequences.

A word here about visitors when you are not present: Suppose a friend of yours wants to stop by and drop off a book at your home while you are at the grocery. Your golden retriever doesn't know your friend and is loose in the house. Do not put your dog in the position of being aggressive toward your friend, no matter how friendly your golden is. Make plans for your friend to come by when you are at home, or make arrangements to put your dog in his crate or in a closed room when you leave and before your friend opens the door.

Exercise Four: Door Control

Door control is a subject that's impossible to ignore for very long. After your pup has reached the independent age of, say, about sixteen to twenty-four weeks, he sees open doors as gateways to stimulation. It doesn't matter whether you're talking about the front door of the house, a backyard gate, or a car door. When it begins to swing open, most dogs want to be the first to cross the threshold.

We tackle this issue on the first hour of the first training day at the center, usually connected to the walking exercise, but not always.

The handler needs to view the newly exposed threshold as an intangible barrier that the dog cannot cross without permission. This exercise also acts as an introduction to perimeter respect (unfenced yards and camping areas). Permission can be given in two different ways: a command or signal for the dog to cross with the handler ("walk" or "heel" for example) or a command or signal for the dog to cross without the handler (like "outside" or "inside"). **But regardless of the *reason* for crossing the threshold, the dog must *wait* until signaled; even if the doorway is standing wide open for an extended period of time.**

At the training center, we shy away from using containment commands such as *sit* and *stay*. This tends to muddy the water around a clear and simple obligation for the dog: Don't cross a newly exposed threshold without the handler's permission). For example, if you tell your dog to sit or stay when you open a door and he chooses to break the command and run across the threshold, then when you correct him with leash and collar is that for breaking the command or bolting out of the doorway? Which responsibility will register as most important in the dog's mind? Keep your training approach simple so that the commands are clear for both handler and companion.

If an owner feels compelled to signal a dog not to cross a threshold, I suggest developing a casual command like "wait" which to my dog means go no farther. With this less rigid command, the handler will not need to concern himself with an official release.

At the onset of this lesson, we supply at least minimal realism and stimulation. We will typically approach our first training door or gate with the dog on a leash (loose of course), leash in hand, allowing our new friend enough length to easily dart through the opening. Jingling keys, knocking on the door, ringing a doorbell, or rattling a gate hasp will create all the stimulation or realism you need at first. Later on, we supply visitors with dogs and food on the other side of the door or fumble with a lawn mower or garbage can at the backyard gate.

Train for realism.

Anticipating the dog's pushing his nose through the first available crack in the doorway, the handler should be ready to administer the necessary leash correction (not restraint or pull) to turn the dog's attention from the doorway to the handler. Assuming you are successful, close the door, then restimulate (by knocking, jingling keys, etc., as before). Then open the door further, ever ready to hand out the appropriate consequences (leash check or praise) depending on the dog's action. Make sure you're timely with soothing and calming praise (we don't need more stimulation at doorways) at the very first signs of self-restraint in your friend.

What we're shooting for is an automatic reaction from the dog. Upon fully opening the door, the dog should look at the handler or, at the very least, contain himself with no use of leash or commands. I am talking about the handler's standing in front of (but not blocking in any way) a fully exposed threshold with attractions of any kind on the other side for as long as he likes with no forward motion from the dog.

As soon as you can count on this kind of control, you should begin practicing with the leash out of hand. Safe doorways should be a priority when hands-off training commences, regardless of a dog's dependability when the leash is in hand. Examples of safe doors would be doors to a fenced backyard, doors to a closed attached garage, or doorways to screened porches or gated decks. If none exist in your home environment, a traditional training long line must be utilized. Depending on the risk of escape, given the dog in training or risk of injury if the dog were to rush through the opening, the long line can be loose on the floor or anchored securely to a doorknob or a piece of heavy furniture as long as there is enough slack in the line that it doesn't serve as a tether and restrain the dog from making his mistakes. Success and safety should be a handler's priorities.

By the time a handler gets to hands-off application in this lesson, he can combine the elements of visitor control by setting up what we call a living room scenario.

Utilizing a safe doorway, designate a small living room accessed by this door for both handler and dog. Casually hang out in the area with the dog on a leash or long line out of hand. Behave normally, reading or watching television with no commands for the dog. Remember, hang out normally! Wait for your prepared visitor (helper) to ring or knock at the door. Casually answer the door, first with your focus on the dog and his door control.

Just like in a real visiting situation, your dog is allowed to accompany you to the door. Take your time! Handle this exercise in distinct steps. First, fully open the door with confidence. Show your dog that you are in control of this situation. If your dog immediately runs out to greet the visitor, step on his leash and give him a couple of tugs back across the threshold and repeat this step.

Let's assume the second time the two of you answer the door, your companion hangs with you while the door stands fully open. After a bit of soothing praise, chat with the visitor for a while, the two of you on opposite sides of the threshold. The visitor should be encouraged to speak to the dog while the dog all the while maintains his composure on the handler's side of the doorway. Once the handler and dog are comfortable with this part of the exercise, move on to step two. Without addressing the dog (but with enough attention directed towards him to effectively train him), the handler should step across the threshold to greet and shake hands with the visitor. If your four-legged friend walks out the door with you (and he will the first couple of times), immediately take hold of his leash and tug him back across to the proper side and repeat the maneuver. Each subsequent time you step out to greet the visitor and your little buddy follows, apply stronger tugs as he is returned to his side of the threshold. It is every bit as important for the handler to leave his visitor to go back and lavishly praise the dog the first time he holds on his own side of the threshold.

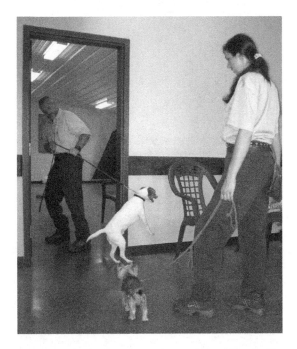

The handler needs to be persistent when enforcing threshold control.

This is probably the most difficult aspect of door control. But this is really where the rubber meets the road. Every dog owner should be able to step out onto the porch and pay the pizza man or accept a delivery. Every dog owner should be able to prop the front door open and help family and friends carry in gifts and food at the holidays. Every dog owner should be able to load or unload the vehicle with their dog patiently waiting to get in or get out.

Remember, our main goal with the exercise is to convince our dog that a tangible barrier is not necessary to secure a threshold. Our door control training is very similar to pet containment system training. The difference is that rather than the buried signal wire triggering an electric collar bite when the dog attempts to cross a boundary, a handler utilizes a leash and collar instead.

Practice managing congestion at doorways.

As difficult as this part of door control training is, a handler and dog should master this before the final step of inviting the guest in. You must be stubborn and hold a hard line on this exercise. Don't allow your little buddy to cheat by sticking his nose across the threshold. Our rule is that not even a toenail or a whisker can pierce that threshold plane.

Remember too that we use no threats or warnings to back the dog from the doorway. **Take action always, be as firm as necessary, but always be pleasant and positive. Convince your dog that regardless of the challenges you face, the two of you are always in good standing.** And don't forget, any investment made in genuine praise and reward for your dog's efforts will always come back to you with dividends.

I hope it will boost your confidence to know that hundreds of dogs a year accomplish this exercise at the training center. We get every imaginable breed of all ages and all backgrounds and not one of them is a lick better than your dog.

Having said all this, invite your helper into the living area and shift your focus to visitor control as you usher your helper to a waiting chair. By now, as you would expect, increase the intensity of the experience (by adding a dog, food, or other visitors) as the dog's proficiency increases. Always try to eventually take the training experience beyond what you would encounter in real life so that little training is needed when it's not officially dog training time and the *real* Aunt Mary has come to visit.

At the training center, all of our basic obedience dogs need to be able to handle this hands-off living room scenario before we consider their instruction complete.

One last bit of discussion on this topic centers around the thresholds of cage openings or doors that mostly remain open. It is my opinion that giving your dog the freedom to cross these types of thresholds does not deteriorate a handler's control over his companion when dealing with typical entryways or exits.

On the flip side of this coin, if an owner would like to establish a rule not to cross into this area even though the doorway remains open, the same approach is used here as for the front door of the house.

Let's say for example we have a nursery or a formal living room whose doorway remains open, yet we do not want the dog in these areas without explicit permission. Approach the doorway as you would the front door but don't cross the threshold. Allow the dog enough leash to cross if he chooses. If he does, check him with your leash and collar sufficiently enough to back him out. When he backs out and contains himself, soothe him with praise. No commands are used here either.

Next, the handler takes one or two steps into the room, again checking the dog until he backs out should the dog choose to cross also. Do not praise the dog until you have returned to his side of the threshold, taking as much time as you like to do so. This is a key to success during this experience: Make the dog wait for your return to receive his reward. As he becomes more proficient, drop the leash and spend longer and longer in the designated area.

Remember, the dog is not on a stay. He can move about as long as he does not cross the threshold into the designated area. If he does break down and cross that invisible barrier, whether you're in the room or not, don't tell him to get out and don't call him. Calmly take hold of the leash and check him all the way out of the area.

No need to be scary or mean, ever! Just be matter-of-fact. If your little buddy sticks his nose into the beehive, sting him. If, on the other hand, he demonstrates self-restraint as you walk past or into the area, offer him a little honey. The honey goes a long way in making the self-control worthwhile for your little buddy.

Given the difficulty of these last several exercises, I can see how a new handler might be inclined to skip portions or move past them altogether. Also, they are not very dramatic. You spend an hour with your dog and have taught him to do nothing but stay calm. But I firmly believe that there is little hope for real control over any dog outside a sterile environment (meaning a training area with no other dogs or people) without this intensive distraction conditioning based on the dog's self-control. That is why we begin all of our obedience training here.

Once a dog has developed composure around distractions and true focus on the handler under normal environmental conditions, the formal commands come easily. Try not to be too hard on yourself during training. These are challenging lessons and mistakes happen. Seldom do these mistakes result in substantial setbacks. You don't have to be perfect to be effective!

Again, any of the sections in this book that involve great detail in setup or exact handling technique should be reread and reread until the information seems clear and familiar.

Exercise Five: Walking

The walking exercise is second to none in developing a follow-the-leader relationship with your dog. I can watch a dog properly walking alongside his handler on the other side of a football field, and I can know that the person has very good control over his dog without ever seeing the two work as a team through formal obedience commands.

The essence of this walking lesson for the dog is to follow the leader (you) regardless of pace, direction, or distraction. In a nutshell, the dog only has two conditions to satisfy: **He must remain on your general left, and he must travel with a slack full leash.**

The purpose of this exercise is to give a person an opportunity to develop handler awareness in his dog and at the same time create a casual but controlled mode of travel. By giving a dog access to a full loose leash (four to six feet) and allowing him to travel anywhere left of the handler's centerline (an imaginary line running between the handler's legs) the dog will be able to travel long distances and not exhaust himself mentally from heavy concentration as he would with the formal heeling command.

Under this informal command, *walk* (and we typically use this one word as a verbal cue to begin this exercise), the dog should be allowed to look around freely and smell the flowers if he wishes, as long as he maintains a loose leash and remains left of the centerline while he does it.

The handler picks the spot for elimination.

We do not allow our dogs to eliminate while we are in the process of walking. We may walk to a designated elimination area, but there are no bathroom breaks along the way. Here are the main reasons for the policy. First and foremost, allowing the dog to eliminate during the walk whenever the urge strikes puts him in control of when you stop and when you start and in most cases where you walk because he is going to be determined to follow his nose. Secondly, giving the dog permission to relieve himself while you walk misdirects his focus from the handler to other dogs and territory marking (both urination and defecation) which very quickly becomes an obsession. Lastly, it simply isn't necessary for your dog to eliminate in the neighbors' yards, on the sidewalks, and along the walking paths in public parks. This practice makes cleanup difficult if not impossible.

As much of a dog person as I am, I have very little tolerance for stepping in dog scat wherever it may be left, in my yard or at the park. And I think most of us would agree that the pungent aroma of dog urine is better left in designated areas than on car tires and park benches. I think all of us dog owners should practice better elimination etiquette so that dogs become more welcome in public places rather than more restricted.

So give your companion a chance to relieve himself before you strike out on a walk and you shouldn't have to worry about any more elimination until you return, even if you intend to cover a half a dozen miles or more.

If you are an apartment or town-house dweller, designate a bathroom area for your dog that's close to home so that it is practical to access in bad weather and on busy mornings. The last thing any busy person needs on a cold, rainy November morning is a long walking ritual with a dog simply to encourage elimination.

If, however, your dog should defecate while you are out for a walk, be a good citizen and clean up after him. This way, you are much more likely to get a wave and a hello from the neighbors when you walk past rather than dirty looks and "Keep OFF the Grass" signs.

When we teach the walking exercise at the training center, we usually end up with some semblance of a casual controlled walk (with a brand-new dog and handler) by the end of the first lesson.

Select a relatively large, flat, and unobstructed training area for this lesson, like a backyard or unfinished basement. As soon as proficiency allows, cruise the neighborhood or the park. One of the keys to success with a new dog, especially a charged-up fellow, is to travel very slowly (as if you have a sprained ankle) at first. You can speed up or vary the speed with proficiency.

Develop the walk with one dog at a time, later on, handle two.

Actually, begin the training session by gripping the leash with two hands, allowing the dog sufficient leash length (four to six feet) for comfortable yet controllable travel. Make sure your hands are touching each other when gripping the leash, the way you would hold a baseball bat. This greatly improves strength and coordination when developing your training technique.

With hands held against the chest (heart area), select a destination. Aim for anything that will help you travel in a straight line. Straight lines are important because they ensure that the dog is unable to influence direction. Remember, the handler always establishes pace and direction while keeping the dog on a loose leash and left of the centerline.

Once the command *walk* is given, 95 percent of the handler's focus should be directed toward the dog. To maintain sustained visual contact and unbroken concentration, use peripheral vision to see where you are going. Don't talk to other people while you are working through the walking lesson. Don't stop to wonder what the dog is thinking as you develop this follow-the-leader relationship. Concentrate only on the two conditions the dog must meet while you walk slowly and steadily toward your target: Your dog stays left of the centerline, and your dog keeps the leash slack.

Here is how you direct the dog into the proper position using the loose leash:

Let's first assume we're dealing with an eager beaver Airedale who wants to charge out at the slightest hint of a walk and lead the way. At the training center, we frequently have to deal with some real wall climbers that dart back and forth just in anticipation of a walk. It's extremely difficult for the handler not to crash to the ground from dizziness just watching.

Lean into your direction change and maintain your balance.

Regardless of the dog's speed and determination, allow him all of the loose leash. As soon as your dog commits to lead in any direction, very quickly and very quietly spin to your right 180 degrees (exactly the opposite direction the dog is charging toward) with your hands gripping the leash locked against the chest, drive toward a new target while preparing for the impact of Speedy Gonzales running out of leash.

The handler during this very moment is defining for the dog that the dog is not the leader (and it's impossible to follow when you're leading) and that the handler is the most important thing the dog can focus on. If we can't accomplish this with our dog, there is little point moving into more formal commands because we will not have the dog's full attention or respect.

I'm going to suppose that with the first 180-degree change in direction that the handler wins the day and the dog is spun around end for end, only to gather his bearings and charge past the handler to lead toward the new destination, whatever that might be. (Most dogs don't care where they are going as long as they get to lead.) Given this outcome, the handler should immediately repeat this process of the quick turn, fully expecting the dog once again to abruptly run out of leash. Only this time, we generally see a significant change in the dog's focus (toward the handler) and a definite slowdown in the dog's eagerness to lead. If not, repeat the 180-degree turn from the dog until he decides that it's best to wait and see what the handler wants to do.

Now we're going to imagine that our walking partner darts behind our back or between our legs, crossing the dreaded centerline.

The handler's immediate response should be to **pull the leash tightly around the left thigh** and thwart the dog's attempt to disrupt or redirect the walk. At this point in the lesson, the handler should view himself as a train on a track. The dog should not be allowed to influence the train in any way. Do not allow the dog to speed you up or slow you down *at all!* Even if he tries to tangle you into a dance by running between your legs, trap him in his effort. **This is done by tightening the leash around your left thigh and using your leg and arm to scissor step to the left all the while keeping the leash taunt against your leg.** Your consistent pulling of the leash forces the dog out from between your legs and back across the centerline and into proper position as you walk along at the same slow speed toward your destination. Note that the leash will slacken again immediately once the dog is back over the centerline on your left where he belongs.

Move slowly but strongly through the scissor step.

Make certain as the leader of your handler-dog team you have a definite direction to walk in. It would be detrimental to the walking plan to allow the dog to influence our direction of travel, even inadvertently. So don't just wander around the training area. Demonstrate with positive confidence that you have a purpose for what you do. In truth, this idea is the main point of the walking lesson: Show the dog he must follow. Even though there's not room for two leaders on your team, the dog will still have a great deal of fun on the walks (with all the stimulation around) especially if you remain lighthearted and try to have fun during the exercise. A good handler should always be on the lookout, especially in early training, for those micro moments when a dog first makes an effort to figure out what it is you want him to do. As soon as you recognize an effort, praise your buddy lavishly and identify for him what he is doing by repeating the command *walk*: "Good boy. Walk."

Often, with a challenging dog, I will stop in mid-track and offer the dog a food bonus and some petting while giving him a needed break from concentration and stress.

If you find yourself dealing with a reluctant walker, a dog that doesn't want to move at all, or maybe a dog who is pulling away and rearing back against the leash out of defiance, don't fall into a tug-of-war confrontation. Instead, lurch ahead toward your destination, tugging and releasing the leash as you slowly move along.

Always be on the alert for the one or two steps of reluctant but compliant travel. Just as soon as you witness that loose leash, even if it's accidental on the dog's part, *stop* and deliver some form of praise along with a repeat of the command *walk*.

Throughout this entire process, you should practice minimal but meaningful communication with your dog, until it's no longer an effort of concentration for him and you. I think it's good practice to make only short treks at first, regardless of whether we're working with a defiant tortoise or a determined hare.

I should mention here that there's no room for handler disappointment or true correction for the dog at this stage of training. We are assuming our dog is brand new to this idea of follow-the-leader with a loose leash, left of the handler's centerline. So there is no way we can consider the dog disobedient when he strikes off in the direction that best suits him. Trying to lead the way has been a natural pattern on walks up to this lesson of enlightenment.

It makes absolutely no difference at what age you begin this walking exercise (over the age of sixteen weeks). It matters not how long you've walked your dog in a different manner or how long you've known this dog. All dogs can be taught to follow the leader.

Keeping a dog left of the centerline on a loose leash can be a frustrating business at first, especially with a determined, fast-moving dog. But remember, all dogs are *capable* of walking politely on the left if no other alternative is offered. At the training center, we teach *walk* to a few hundred dogs a year, every breed imaginable, all ages, all sizes, males and females, with every possible temperament. I'm quite sure we've come across every challenge that can come up, and we've overcome all these obstacles using the technique I just introduced.

One of the best techniques we utilize at the training center for reinforcing yield to the handler is turning against a wall. This technique galvanizes the idea of giving way to the leader.

Move slowly into and along the wall, using the leash to help force the dog to reverse direction.

Yielding to a handler's left turns is a critical idea in this walking relationship. A dog must be taught that as the handler turns into him, he must give way or back up, not circle around front, push into, or climb on. In other words, when a handler turns left on a casual walk, the dog must be attentive enough to also turn left.

I believe there is more at stake here than just comfortable travel. A dog that fails to yield easily on left turns is also a dog that has not completely bought into the "Yes, ma'am/sir" idea. I see this reluctance to give way on left turns as a reflection of the dog's lack of respect for the handler. And there's no better way to address it than by compelling a dog to give way on these left turns while remaining on the proper side of the centerline.

When you begin practicing left turns, travel very slowly so that you can safely and successfully walk into the dog, scuffing his toes with your toes and bumping his chin or shoulder with your knees or shins (depending on the size of the dog), forcing him to back up and turn left. Use your leash all that you need in this process by shortening and checking outward to your left (the desired direction for the dog), but nothing works better than your legs against his body and especially your toes against his toes.

Do not allow your companion to turn this exercise into a dance that he controls. If he climbs up on you, keep moving, scuffing his back toes and bumping his chest. Or use your leash to check him off you, but keep slowly moving left.

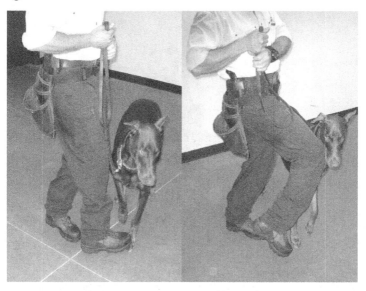

Lightly drag your feet across the floor when scuffing the dog's toes. Use just enough bump with your knee to drive the dog back.

If your dog tries to outmaneuver you by jumping in front or running around you, draw in your leash and swing him back in place as you keep on track the best you can. It is paramount in this exercise that we convince the dog that he cannot affect our course of action. As always, look for opportunities to soothe and praise while you walk through this process. Your dog is a friend. Try not to lose sight of that while forging this follow-the-leader relationship. Remember, it's a game, a game that you will win sooner rather than later. And the walking exercise can actually be fun, especially if you look at it as a contest. I do!

I usually tackle this concept with the dog in lesson one, just as soon as I have the dog's attention and have coaxed him into following along. The approach is simple. Walk very slowly with your dog parallel to an unobstructed stretch of an interior or exterior wall so that the dog is between you and the wall on your left side, no more than two of the dog's body widths between your left shoulder and the wall. (A length of chain-link or privacy fence instead of a wall works well, too.) Leading with the right leg, turn 180 degrees into the wall, just in front of your dog's nose so that you are now walking in the other direction, and the dog's proper position is on your left, away from the wall. Your dog likely will not move into his proper position but will instead block your progress. Move into the dog with your right shoulder actually against the wall, and work your way along the wall, bumping your knees into the dog's nose and chest while scuffing his toes with your feet. You must keep driving into the dog, up the wall until the dog yields by backing out of the way to your left. To gain anything from this exercise, a handler must not stop until the dog yields and the way is clear for the handler to choose another direction. Make sure at first you execute this technique very slowly so that stumbling, stepping on the dog, or failing to progress forward are not options. If you happen to run out of wall or fence, which sometimes happens with strong, determined dogs, persist alongside furniture and if you have to, navigate corners. Don't hurt yourself or the dog, but forcing a yield here is critical in developing a leadership role with your dog. You will probably find out just how important this exercise is when you experience your dog's determination not to give ground.

I can't help but admire most dogs and their tenacity to win or influence. I believe any handler will have greater success if he views this exercise as a game or a challenge. One aspect of the game is trying to set up the dog by using interesting targets as destinations, then attempting to sneak away by pivoting to the right and taking the leash with you. The dog's goal of course is to avoid being sucked in by the sirens and so he must watch the handler closely so there is no sneaking away.

The other aspect of this game is attempting to catch the dog off guard with sharp (but not rushed) left turns, bumping and scuffing into our challenger, forcing him to back up and give way. The dog's challenge here is to be so attentive and quick of foot that he yields every time without allowing for any contact.

When a handler finds that he can no longer catch his dog off guard— when no matter the speed he travels or how many times he changes direction, no matter how many distractions are about, his dog is left of the centerline on a loose, full leash—the training has been successful.

We have covered a great deal of important material in this section. In essence, I just described how to establish yourself as the leader with your dog without using heavy-handed techniques or emotional negativity. Be sure to reread this section before you begin your first walking lesson.

The Formal Commands

People who love soft words and hate iniquity forget this, that reform consists in taking a bone away from a dog. Philosophy will not do this.

—John Jay Chapman (1862–1933)

Our basic philosophy of positive, calm, focused, and firm handling that I've outlined during the good manners instruction is equally important in formal command training. Our concentration in this section, however, will be on the development of a specific response from the dog to a specific signal. The five formal commands we'll consider are these: *heel, sit, down, stay,* and *come.*

In this book, we are not concerned with a competition style of response which would be exact and animated. However, we are going to train for an immediate and dependable response from the dog to a single command. Our goal is to end up with both handler and dog being comfortable and confident about their formal command relationship.

There are three aspects to this training process that will apply to all five formal commands. These are teaching, reinforcing, and proofing. Before you tackle even the first aspect of the first command, be certain that your dog has mastered the first five exercises so completely that you and he can work without a leash. This will ensure smooth sailing through the formal commands, because in the process of developing good manners, the dog has learned to control his drives and energy, he has learned to defer to the handler before making decisions, and he has also learned how to concentrate in the midst of distractions. That is why, at my training center, we consider manners to be the primary concern of basic obedience with formal commands a close second.

At a beginners' seminar for inexperienced handler-dog teams, I don't even discuss formal commands except to say that we launch from good manners into formal training so that we can minimize resistance in the dog and frustration in the handler when tackling the challenges of the more specific responses associated with obedience commands. With any of my training programs, the goal is always the same: Make the learning process a positive process for both the handler and the dog.

Let's begin our formal training with aspect one of command one: teaching the *heel*.

Exercise Six: Heel

Since the development of the heeling position is so similar to the development of the walking position, I've covered this exercise as the first formal command. The stationary placement commands of *sit, down,* and *stay* will follow, leaving *come* as the final and most challenging directive to be developed.

The optimal way for a handler to view the heeling exercise is simply as the formal version of walking. ***Heel* is essentially a position a dog must maintain in relation to his handler; specifically, the right side of the dog's neck should be about nine inches from the outside of the handler's left leg.**

The dog needs to heel close to the handler for safety, but the actual distance is an approximation.

Why the left side? It's most convenient for a right-handed society. The left hand can control the dog while the right hand is free to shake or manage doors, phones, and babies. The left side is the safest place for the dog to be when walking against traffic (by law). Most untrained dogs are walked on the right side because it usually correlates with the strong arm of the handler which is needed to restrain the pulling of their untrained companion. Train the dog, remove the pulling, and the left side of the handler usually becomes the most convenient place for the dog.

We instruct new handlers in our training lessons to imagine plugging their left thumb in the outer seam of their left pant while at the same time plugging their left little finger into the dog's collar. This verbal description often helps a new handler visualize the dog's responsibility in terms of radius to handler or, in other words, the dog's obligatory heeling position. Keep in mind: neck close to leg is good; neck against leg is not. During the heeling exercise, just as in the walking exercise, the handler should be able to move about unimpeded regardless of pace or changes in direction.

The impetus behind the development of the formal *heel* command is safety and precision. We already have convenience in handling and easy travel from our walking exercise, but because we allow the dog a generous radius of three to six feet when casually traveling, we lack optimal control in congested areas or tight quarters. For example, when strolling through the park with our dog for fun and physical exercise, we would choose the *walk* command to allow our companion the freedom to enjoy the surroundings and the experience. *Walk* again would be the preferred command when taking our friend out for elimination, affording him the relaxed mind-set needed for relief. On the other hand, when crossing a busy street, we choose the command *heel* to keep our dog close to our leg for safety, allowing for quick starts and stops. *Heel* would also be the appropriate command when entering a veterinarian's waiting room, making it possible for the handler and the dog to weave around the sick and unruly dogs.

Heeling requires so much more concentration and effort from the dog (because his obligated radius is so short) that a handler should never require his dog to heel for long distances or stretches of time. It would be unfair to expect our companions to maintain such an exact position for extended periods. In fact, your dog will mentally fatigue if you push for long heeling durations, and he won't be able to maintain an accurate position.

Remember, we need accuracy for precision and safety. If you find yourself in a situation where your dog needs to heel a lot, give him as many short breaks as possible, even if that means finding a quiet spot to stop and briefly release him with some reward. **My advice is to use the walking command whenever possible (which is why we teach it) and preserve the more accurate heeling command for the times when you need it.**

The training process for the heeling command begins with the walk command. It is a good idea to warm your dog up to formal training with a few minutes of walking which will heighten his handler awareness and help him channel his energy before we expect him to really concentrate. At the training center, we find that it's good practice to warm up all of our dogs with loose-leash walking before every formal command training session. The warm-up helps ensure the dog will have a positive formal command experience because his drive is already in control. He's deferring to the handler and managing distractions going into the more demanding formal instruction.

With the dog already in the walking position from the warm-up, step toward him so that the outside of your left leg lines up with the right side of his neck about nine inches apart (in other words, the heeling position). As you move into this position, collect your leash so that it's kept off the ground, out from under the legs, loose and in control. Think of your right thumb as a hanger. During the walking exercise, we usually only have the leash handle hanging in the right thumb with the balance of the leash dangling free at the dog's disposal. Since the heeling exercise will demand the dog to maintain no more than about nine inches of obligated radius, (assuming you're training with a standard four- to six-foot leash), **we're left with excess that should hang neatly in a single loop on the same right thumb.**

Maintain a short but loose leash with a comfortable, firm grip.

This loop of excess should overlay the leash handle which was already hanging there from the walking exercise. Ideally, the leash should be gripped with both hands beginning with the right thumb at the top with the right hand below followed by the left hand below the left thumb. Both hands should wrap around all layers of the leash as if you were gripping a baseball bat. Carry your hands close to your belt buckle allowing for enough leash length (between hands and collar) that your dog can move about the heeling vicinity with no sensation of restriction. Our goal is not to hold the dog in the heeling position but to teach him through consequences to watch us closely enough that he maintains an approximate nine-inch radius (neck to leg) by maneuvering on a loose leash. Keep in mind that the leash length needs to be short enough (hands to collar) that a tight leash correction can be given by pulling the hands from the belt buckle to just below the shoulder line with no grip adjustment.

The end result of proper heeling instruction is to convey to the dog that he's responsible for maintaining this position (when the *heel* command is given) with no leash or handler help at all. This exercise is not unlike the walk. It's simply closer to the handler and therefore requires more concentration and exactness on the dog's part. Remember that walking is for casual travel, and heeling is for formal travel, but both should develop into leash-free exercises.

With the handler and the dog now in relative position one to another, with the leash secure and the grip set, we're ready to teach the dog what heel means (the first aspect of the first command).

Say pleasantly to the dog, "Heel." Then start off with the left foot (no hurry), traveling just a short distance. Watch your dog the entire time! Travel slowly. If the dog makes any effort (even accidentally) to maintain this close position while you're moving, tell him, "Good boy. Heel," while you continue to travel. If your dog fails to travel in this close position or if he strays beyond the approximate nine-inch radius allowed, give him light, encouraging leash tugs (in the appropriate direction) right away without saying anything. Continue traveling and administering the necessary encouraging tugs until your dog is compelled to move into the heeling position while you're moving.

Tug and release on heeling corrections. Do not drag!

Just as soon as your dog reaches the desired position, cease the tugging, making sure your hands are returned to the belt buckle position affording him a loose leash. At the moment your dog moves into the heeling spot, praise him and repeat the *heel* command one time. Keep in mind the handler should be traveling through this entire process, gaze directed toward the dog. While you move along, reward your dog for any efforts to comply and be quick to quietly tug if his efforts stray. All the while, use the *heel* command sparingly, only to begin the exercise with, or to emphasize proper loose-leash position when the dog has returned from straying. Along those same lines, a dog's name should only be used sparingly to engage the dog's attention prior to putting him in drive with a command or in association with praise. The dog's name or the command should never be repeated simply to hold his attention during an exercise. This only transfers the responsibility of focus and concentration from the dog to the handler, pushing the handler-dog relationship in exactly the opposite direction we intended from the onset of training. Besides, we want the dog's name and all commands to hold real value. If we make a habit of unnecessary repetition of those important words, their value will be greatly and immediately diminished.

The second aspect of developing the *heel* command, reinforcing, commences the very moment a dog demonstrates he is working to maintain this close position to the handler with minimal leash use even though there are changes in pace and direction. When we work on heeling at the training center, although we stay at an overall slow speed, we begin 90-degree turns, figure eights, and changes in pace right away.

We want to convey to the dog that the word *heel* means challenge. As a handler, I want to travel on a route that forces the dog to focus closely on me. During the reinforcing aspect of this command, we assume the dog has a crystal-clear understanding of his heeling obligation (keep your collar within about nine inches of my left leg, regardless of pace or direction changes, without any help from me, the handler). Our canine companions have a tall order to fill with this command indeed, so be sure your teaching was done thoroughly and completely before you place the entire heeling responsibility on your partner's shoulders.

If you have any doubts about your dog's understanding of his heeling obligation, spend more time slowly and carefully working him into position and put a great deal of importance on the praise when he makes the effort to be in place. Keep telling yourself there's no race to get finished. This is supposed to be a positive learning experience.

In fact, it's best to ease into this reinforcing by gradually turning up the heat on the leash tugs anytime your partner strays from position. Remember, even as your tugs increase in intensity, there's no need for reprimands or negative emotions. Just like the light teaching tugs, there are no additional commands associated with the stronger reinforcement tugs. All we are really doing at this stage of training is supplying a more substantial negative consequence for our dog's decision not to cooperate for the incentives of praise, a loose leash, and optional food rewards for responding to his new obligations.

I want to stress here that throughout this entire *heel* training process there is no dragging the dog or tug-of-war. There is only continuous movement forward on the handler's part with repeated tugs and releases as necessary to encourage the dog to remain close to the handler during this exercise.

If a handler drags his partner along, the dog has no chance to recover from the negative leash consequence and reconsider his options to cooperate. If a handler stops forward progress to engage his canine companion in tug-of-war, the dog is in control of this dance and the handler is not moving along as planned. With a resistant dog, the plan is to continuously travel while tugging and releasing, all the while concentrating on our friend's responses, looking for any opportunity to praise him even for the slightest effort in the right direction. This is the same objective we had for *walk*; the only difference is that the length of the radius allowed for *heel* is much shorter and therefore more difficult for the dog to maintain.

It is worth mentioning again: Practice heeling in short bursts. Heeling is challenging. Keep the sessions brief.

As you move along through heeling reinforcement, make your practice courses gradually more demanding. Look for distractions your dog can heel around. Incorporate more dramatic changes in pace and direction, all the while encouraging the dog to maintain his close position by utilizing the incentives and deterrents. Always think of keeping a balanced training relationship with your dog. The stronger the leash tugs become with reinforcement, the more rewarding the praise must become. The more challenging the training session becomes, the more breaks are needed.

How long should a formal training session be? The answer to this question depends so much of course on all the variables of a particular training relationship, like the experience of the handler, age of the dog, type of instruction, experience of the canine student, and environmental conditions. For the purposes of this book, considering that most readers and their canine students will be neophytes, I would suggest that training sessions last no longer than fifteen to thirty minutes to cover warm-up as well as all the teaching, reinforcing, and distraction proofing of the various commands being worked on in that particular training session. Remember also that soothing or stimulating interaction time with the dog should be included in each training session. I have found that the busier the dog and handler are during those fifteen- to thirty-minute sessions, the more productive they will be. I have found over the last twenty-seven years that most handlers cover way too little in their typical training session and that the session runs way too long.

Use imagination to create a distracting environment.

The final aspect of training is the distraction-proofing phase of our first formal command. To me, this is always the most enjoyable part of training. The expressions we witness on some of the dogs' faces are almost human. The most expressive dogs look up at us as if to say, "You can't be serious. You expect me to heel right through that garbage? No dog can heel past that barking Pekinese without losing control, can they? I'm not heeling over that pizza, and you can't make me. Can you?"

There is only one purpose behind distraction proofing and that is that in real life, you and your dog will encounter many unplanned distractions. If training doesn't work in the real world, it simply doesn't work at all. If you cannot count on your dog's response in a natural environment (as opposed to the artificially controlled training environment), you cannot count on your dog's response, period.

During the teaching and reinforcing stages of training, it is very helpful for both dog and handler to work in a relatively sterile (meaning distraction-free) and controlled area. This helps to facilitate a relaxed and positive atmosphere so that clear thinking and absorption will define the learning experience. But now we assume we've laid the proper foundation for this heeling command (as we will for the remaining four formal commands) with careful teaching and patient reinforcement in a more forgiving environment. Let's slowly progress into the less forgiving real world.

As always, try not to overwhelm your canine friend. Introduce inanimate non-odiferous objects (such as furniture and toys) as your first distractions to heel around, next to, and over. Next, set up a plate of food and an open garbage pail as figure-eight posts (about ten feet apart). Start off heeling with slow, wide turning eights around the posts then gradually pick up the pace and tighten the turns. Use your imagination to set up realistic training exercises. For example, heel up to the front door of your home, ring the doorbell, and have someone invite you inside. Heel into and throughout the house. Arrange to meet a friend walking her dog on a sidewalk away from home. Heel up to your friend and shake hands. Address each other's dogs before you heel on your way, passing each other dog to dog. Be careful when you practice around vehicle traffic. Some dogs can become extremely startled at the sight or sound of certain vehicles, presenting the handler with a sometimes surprising emotional reaction that the handler didn't count on.

Heeling with two is like heeling with one.

Sooner than you think, it will be time to heel to a real park-like atmosphere and all the unpredictable distractions that go along with it. Be choosy when selecting the first uncontrolled public setting. Scout out your site in advance before taking your dog. We want real life at this point, but we would also like for the experience to be manageable. Minimal uncontrolled dogs and children would be nice, along with minimal vehicular traffic for your first public outing.

Wherever you decide to go as your first public training session, make sure as the handler you can concentrate mostly on the dog!

This build-up approach to distraction proofing will be similar for all the commands. And we can't forget that the one main purpose behind all of the obedience training is real-life control. That is the thrust of this book.

Exercise Seven: Sit

On to the next command: sit at your side. Once again, we begin with the teaching aspect. Even if your dog already sits for a treat or usually sits in some fashion on his own time by command, we're going to start from scratch to ensure our four-legged friend understands exactly how, where, and when to sit, following a command. We don't want any of our dogs learning that it's okay to put their own spin on a response. If your dog is truly good at sitting already, then it will be easy sailing through this command.

Assuming that the leash and the collar are attached to the dog, step into the *heel* position so that the right side of the dog's neck is close to your left leg (about nine inches between his collar and your leg). The leash should be securely held in the right hand only allowing just enough length to keep the dog's collar loose when your hand is held below the belt. I do want you to be able to straighten the leash while tightening the collar, moving only the right hand from below the belt to no more than chest height. This action, using the right hand only, will completely control the front end of your dog, allowing the left hand to control his rear end.

The plan is to bring his head up at the same time the rump is pushed down, and all of this is done in one swift, smooth motion that immediately follows the single command or signal *Sit*.

Try to keep your feet in place while firmly yet calmly placing the dog into sit.

Before the sit command is given, the left hand should be at the ready, behind your dog's line of sight and just above his loin. We control the position of the dog's rear end by gripping his lower back with our thumb on the right side of his spine and our four fingers on the left side. Obviously, the strength required and the force needed for placement varies greatly from one dog to another. You will only need fingertips for your Yorkie. If you are training an Irish wolfhound, you could use another set of hands. **However, the objective remains the same: being able to place your dog in the correct sitting position (on his rear feet, not thighs) in the original place we intend (at our left side, no dancing) after a single command *sit.*** This is a tall order indeed if you are not prepared, but you are now!

If a handler wants a dependable, accurate response from his dog each time he gives a command, then he must be prepared to place his canine in the proper position associated with the command or signal given. This result must be connected to the appropriate command over and over again to develop a lasting association in the dog's mind. A handler should be very careful in this teaching stage of training to ensure that there is absolutely no deviation in command or result so the dog's image of this connection is as clear as his trainer's.

Keep in mind there should be no communication with the dog during the actual placement process. The handler should be all about focus and determination. Repeat the command *sit* once the dog has settled into the appropriate posture. Then add some praise.

Once the connection between command and posture clicks in the dog's mind, the teaching phase of training this command is over forever! In truth, the average dog only requires a dozen or so placements with commands to be comfortable with this association. As a trainer, you can always tell when your dog reaches command savvy by the degree of cooperation with the actual placement. With a competent handler and a run-of-the-mill dog, each placement should meet with less resistance until you reach the one magical command where your canine student beats you to the punch in assuming the correct posture. From that very moment, the trainer shifts into reinforcement mode, the second aspect of the training process, and never looks back. If there are any doubts about your dog's clarity in understanding his obligation, keep teaching. You'll not hurt the training process. As your dog's caretaker, you should feel confident and comfortable about moving on to the reinforcing phase of this project.

Reinforcing the *sit* command so that it becomes the dog's sole responsibility to assume the sitting posture within a couple of seconds is the second aspect of training the second formal command. In the reinforcing phase of training, it is paramount to success that the handler be prepared to deliver timely consequences, both positive and negative, depending on a dog's decision to cooperate or not. The entire thrust of this aspect of training is to completely relieve the handler of any placement responsibility.

Remember, it is the dog's responsibility to hold the sit.

So with your dog in the *heel* position (the right side of his neck next to your left side) and your leash held in short lock fashion, give your dog a pleasant *sit* command. There is no need for harshness in the command tone or drill-sergeant-like inflection to show the dog you're serious. The immediate consequence following your dog's decision (to sit or not to sit) will demonstrate your earnestness. Remember, though, you're not asking or hoping that the dog will sit. All of our formal commands should be viewed as directives that are pleasantly delivered.

Keep in the forefront of your mind in this stage of training that the handler no longer instantly places the dog in connection with the command. Teaching is done. Now we must wait (only a moment) to see what the dog chooses to do after the command.

Obedience training is a relationship-building process between handler and dog, centering around three concepts: a dog's self-control over his drives and energy, deference to the handler before action, and distraction management.

Just as soon as the command is given, your dog's response clock begins ticking. Allow him no more than a slow one-one-thousand to commit to his task. Allow him another slow one-one-thousand to complete his task. Giving your dog any more time than this promotes debate over obligation and sloppiness in response. Be careful not to reward your dog before he completes his task or else he may think that a partial sit is good enough or that maybe his handler will jump in and help out. It is just as important to reward your friend the exact moment he assumes the appropriate sitting posture so he knows this is precisely what you had in mind when you gave the command.

Any of our standard rewards work as a positive consequence for the dog's correct decision as long as they're not overly done, creating a disruption in the training process. For example, genuinely soothing or lightly stimulating pats and praise are good. Too much praise and the dog dances out of the sit position forcing the handler to follow the positive response to *sit* with the negative management of this error.

Although unintended, the dog is left with a foul taste in his mouth even though he made an effort in the right direction. The same is true for food reward. Food should be utilized as a bonus only, not as bait for the dog to focus on. If the food is used as bait, the dog will become dependent on it and only respond properly if the bait is present and he is hungry at that moment. Besides, we want the dog to focus on what is really important: his handler's wishes. Therefore, any food used for reward should be out of sight and out of mind for the dog until it is delivered. That's why at the training center we carry our food in a pouch worn in the small of the back or on the right hip, invisible to the dog, yet immediately accessible at the very moment we need it without any fumbling through pockets or packages.

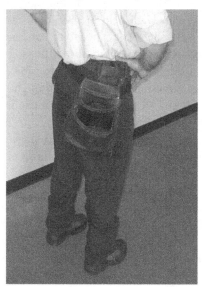

If you use a pouch, make sure you can get your hand in and out easily.

Fumbling for the reward, using too much (this is not a meal!), or having food with inappropriate consistency (crumbly or sticky), all turn the bonus into a disruption. What we have found works best for our training purposes at the center is a fresh, frozen meaty dog food. Although it's a little bit of a hassle to thaw and keep, it is ideal. If you happen to be working with a dog who doesn't have much interest in a food bonus, training is all the easier for you. Simply stick with what works best: a genuine kind word or a touch on the nose or a pat on the shoulder. When it comes to praise or positive consequence, the bottom line is whatever lights the dog's tinder works for us as long as it is not disruptive.

Now let's assume your canine partner did not respond to the directive completely in the time allotted. Since you assumed the working position before the command was given, you should be instantly ready to apply an upward snap with the leash (as opposed to steady upward tension during teaching) and a more forceful grab and downward push on the loin with the left hand (as opposed to steady downward pressure during teaching). The upward angle of the leash should be at about 45 degrees from the floor to minimize backward or forward movement from the dog as the sit is being accomplished. Your left hand should assist in keeping the dog in place while the downward push is taking place. I think it's very important to minimize dancing and wrestling with the dog during this sit exercise in order to convey to our canine partner that there is only one outcome possible with the *sit* command and that is to drop to your hocks right where you are!

Make sure you loosen your leash after each correction.

The force needed with the upward leash snap and the downward shove will vary tremendously from one dog to the next, depending on size, compliance levels, and pain tolerance. Just make sure that you begin with a force that's noticeably stronger than the teaching placement. A handler can always increase the force used during this phase of training if a dog persistently refuses to cooperate and sit within the time allotted.

However, it is more difficult for a handler to reduce the force used once he has startled the dog with too much at the beginning. This is because the heightened nervousness in our rattled canine will obscure his clarity of thought and undermine his trust in his handler. So always begin the reinforcement of a command with the least force you estimate will work and quickly increase as your student requires.

Remember throughout the entire reinforcement process that there is no negative emotion displayed by the handler *at all*! No reprimands, no chastising, no yelling. Negative emotion is never condoned in my training program. That kind of negativity only puts a handler at odds with the partner he is trying to win over.

A good trainer is always calm, focused, positive, and absolutely as firm as necessary. As firm as necessary means the force of placement increases as resistance to *sit* (of the dog's own volition) lingers. However, once the dog has been successfully forced into the proper position, the slack is instantly returned to the leash and the left hand is immediately removed from the dog's loin.

If the dog rises from the sit, swiftly apply upward leash tension (with the right hand) and the downward shove with the left hand grabbing the loin. During the strong placement action of reinforcing, there should be no communication with the dog, just quiet determination on the handler's part.

Just as soon as you have successfully replaced the dog in the sitting posture, confidently but calmly repeat the *sit* command to strengthen the association between the directive and the correct response. Withhold reward until your dog demonstrates that he's on board with the program by holding that posture for a couple of moments with zero help from the handler (this means no leash tension, no threatening hand gestures, and no audible reminders).

Regardless of the amount of effort required to get your dog to hold a command on his own or finally respond to your directive on his own accord, all of the praise given should be genuine. Use real emotion to soothe or lightly stimulate your buddy. Your dog must know always that the two of you are on good terms.

Use genuine praise but do not allow a broken sit.

Now let's say you have worked diligently for several days reinforcing your dog's sit response. It's time for the third and final aspect of training this command: proofing around distractions. In this stage of training, we should purposefully introduce more significant distractions into the working area. For instance, have someone walk through the area within close proximity of the dog at the moment you deliver the *sit* command. You might walk your dog up to a plate of leftover pizza on the floor and have your buddy sit right beside it. At some point, a handler should have another dog walker or helper caring for a cat approach and have the dog sit directly in front of the temptation. Intentionally walk over to a spilled bag of garbage and insist on a proper sit from your dog with his tail to the bag. In each of these situations, the handler's expectation should be the same: an appropriate sit response from the dog following a single command.

Prepare your canine friend for the real world by allowing your imagination to set up more and more challenging scenarios. Be careful in the beginning not to bite off more than you or your partner can chew. Gradually build up realistic situations utilizing people, other animals, strange settings, and food. With careful practice over a period of just days, you will end up with a dependable, accurate response from your dog to a single, pleasant command. You will have truly developed a trained response and not a trick.

A word here about tricks. **If your dog is taught to sit as a trick, it means that the conditions have to be just right before he will cooperate.** Perhaps he will only sit if there is a food reward that he can see as a consequence. **If your dog is *trained* to sit, that means he will cooperate unconditionally when you give him the command.** And that is the kind of behavior we have to have to control our dogs in the real world.

Exercise Eight: Down

Before we move on to our eighth command, *down*, I want to identify the three main purposes of basic obedience in naked terms, because by simplifying and stripping away the formality of obedience commands, as handlers, we are able to maintain clarity in our focus during training. **If we were to boil formal, canine obedience training down to its barest essence or purpose, we would end up with three musts for the dog: 1) the dog must follow the handler, 2) the dog must remain still, and 3) the dog must return to the handler, all on command.**

By keeping these musts in mind while engaged in the process of training, a new handler is much less likely to accept sloppiness like a *nearly* slack leash when walking the dog, a position *pretty* close to the heeling position, a *conditional* stay, or *almost* coming to front and center. If a handler's formal training fails to gain these three musts, accurately and dependably by command, then the handler's formal training will fail. Formal command response is worthless if you can't count on it. At the same time, I would tell you that I don't want a machine for my companion. I want my dog to be the spirited animal that he was intended to be. Of course I want him controlled enough that he can be with me without infringing upon the rights and privileges of others. And that is what basic obedience is all about. I also feel that the approach to canine obedience presented in this book is so natural in feel for both dog and handler, so straightforward and positive, that regardless of whether we're talking about my dog or yours, anyone from family to strangers can enjoy being in the same space with our pets.

The next command we teach is *down*. Again, we begin from the working position with the dog on our left, his right shoulder nearly touching our left leg just as we began the *sit*.

The leash and collar are attached to the dog, and the leash is in hand, of course. **Slide your left hand down the leash towards the dog's collar until the little finger bumps into the leash snap. Your left hand should be closed tightly around the leash with your palm down (it would be facing the floor if the hand were open), and you should be looking down at the back of your hand with the little finger snuggled up close to the right side of the dog's neck.** The balance of the leash can be dropped on the floor in front of your left foot or simply carried in your right hand. I prefer the balance of the leash on the floor because it will not be used during *down* placement.

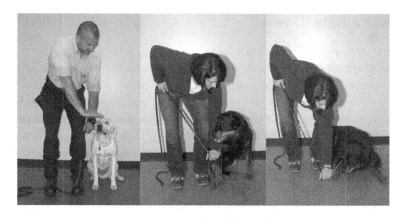

Once you have begun down placement, keep the pressure on the dog until he is relaxed on the floor.

As with all of our training, prior to any forceful action, as the handler, reassure your dog that he's a good fellow. After the brief bit of praise, give your dog a pleasant *down* command. Once you've allowed for the processing moment (about two seconds) following the command, apply steady downward pressure on the collar with the left arm and shoulder. **Keeping the left arm straight and rigid allows a handler to utilize upper torso strength and weight to steadily drop the dog's head to the floor.** Imagine your left arm working as a slow-motion pile driver. Where the dog's head goes, the rest of the body will *eventually* follow. We're in no hurry at this stage of training, remember. Assist with the right hand if you need to (right hand on the leash next to the left) until the dog's chin is at the floor.

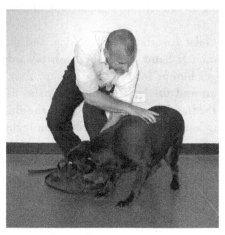

Do not be in a hurry, and have a firm grip on the dog's back.

If your dog's body did not follow his head or if his rear end is dancing away from your left side, use your *right* hand to grab your dog's loin or the base of the withers (right palm across the spine) and push his rear end to the floor along your left side while the left hand continues to hold his chin in place. Keep in mind, even if your dog already understands the *down* command and will comply with insistence or while being led by food, that this placement process is still necessary. It is critical during this teaching process that we convey to the dog in unambiguous terms that there is one command and that he must respond completely and immediately. So after the initial command, the handler should be quiet and concentrate on effective placement.

Once our buddy is in proper position (elbows and hocks on the floor), release the tension on the collar (but don't give up your grip) and release your grip on his loin (but don't remove your hand) and quickly say, "Down. Good boy." When your dog tries to prematurely (before permission) stand up from the *down* position, immediately reposition your dog using no words. After this repositioning, loosen your grip and leash tension and once again repeat, "Down. Good boy." During this teaching stage of *down* placement, release your dog from the prone position after only a moment of his successfully holding that position. Tell your dog he's all done, and encourage him to stand up and shake off any stress associated with the exercise while you lavish him with good stuff.

If you happen to be working with a dog that is particularly resistant to this *down* placement, remember time is on your side. Once the command has been given and you begin placing the dog, don't let up until he is on the floor. **It doesn't matter how long the process takes. Be calm, be persistent, be quiet, and most important, be determined to do it your way.** Every single dog will fatigue in resistance to this *down* placement. And sooner rather than later, every single dog will begin dropping to the floor at the handler's side with the slightest downward tension on the leash or pressure along the back.

Before we leave this teaching phase of training, make sure you can effortlessly place your dog on the floor and he will hold that position while you stand up *straight* with slack leash in hand for up to a full minute. You can pet him occasionally while he holds. You can offer him some praise while he holds, but you can't pressure him into holding.

Make sure your dog is very comfortable with this command before you move on.

We can't forget that during this training process, we're conveying to our dog full responsibility for the *down* position, one good moment after the command is given.

Reinforcement of the *down* response begins as it did with the *sit* command, just as soon as the handler is confident that his dog is clear about and comfortable with his duty. Like with the *sit* exercise, the force and speed of placement is gradually cranked up with the *down* during reinforcement. We want the dog to try to beat us to the punch. We want him to prefer placing himself in the prone posture at our side instead of waiting for our forceful manner, because during reinforcement, our slow motion, left-arm pile driver (used during teaching) becomes a faster, more explosive driver. And the downward pressure of our right hand on our little buddy's back turns more into a shove.

As always, there's no change in communication with the dog moving from teaching to reinforcing. There's never any forceful emotion used: just crisper, more powerful placement along with an abundance of rewards whenever our four-legged friends make efforts in the right direction.

Definitely with this formal *down* command, you can encounter an unusual amount of resistance from an otherwise cooperative fellow, especially in the reinforcement phase of training. The reason behind your dog's resistance tends to center around two ideas as far as the dog is concerned. First of all, when a handler physically puts a dog into a *down* posture on the floor, the handler is bringing into stark reality the fact that the handler is in charge, on top, and dominant. During this exercise, there is no escape from that truth for the dog, especially from his lowly position at the feet of his handler on the floor. The second catalyst for possible uncharacteristic resistance to the *down* command is a dog's overwhelming feeling of being put out of sight, out of mind, and out of the mix of attention when he is placed in that posture.

So there is definitely a correlation between an energized (driven), gregarious, or dominant dog and the dog's resistance to the *down* command. The more in control of an environment a dog feels he is, the more resistant he'll be when forced to give it up. Also, the more driven and social a dog is, the more difficult it is for him to accept the out-of-action responsibility. My feeling is that if I have a problem with my dog over energy control or who's in charge, I would just as soon work it out during this structured exercise as any other time.

The reinforcement phase of training is all about defining authority and responsibility, so try not to shy away from any opportunities! And remember that in this stage of training, a handler should gradually but persistently transfer more and more command response obligation from his shoulders to the dog's. With this formal command, just like the previous two, *pleasant* and *persistent* are two guide words for the handler's approach.

I'm sure by this time the reader can imagine the distraction conditioning for the *down* command is managed almost identically to the reinforcement of *heel* and *sit*. One exception may be the resistance factor encountered with the *down* responsibility. Be doubly sure you have worked out any kinks in your friend's mind about his obligation before you complicate the working environment. If not, the resistance you encountered in teaching or reinforcing this exercise will be increased exponentially with the presence of even a little real-world stimulation.

Exercise Nine: Stay

Once you've prepared your canine partner for the command *down* in real-life situations, it's time to add the all-important *stay* to his repertoire. As I mentioned before, the three main achievements that lie behind formal commands are these: follow, stay, and return. There is hardly a command more important than this one, and there is no better position to apply it in than after a *down* command. Even though as handlers we might couple *stay* with *sit* or ask the dog to remain standing with the *stay* command, *down* allows for the longest stay potential because of its comfortable posture. Therefore, *down* is the most useful posture to couple with *stay*. So for simplicity and the purposes of this book, we will develop the *stay* command from the down position. Keep in mind that the development of *stay* with *sit* is also useful and is carried out in like fashion.

Beginning with the dog in the *down* or *sit* at *heel* position, hold the leash with the left hand only, grasping at about twenty inches above the dog's collar. The handle can be carried in the left hand or simply dropped to the floor. Your left hand should be held nearly against your left hip. After the command and/or signal *stay* is given, allowing for the brief moment of processing, **step fluidly with your right foot (pivoting on your left) all the way around so that you are now directly facing your dog. The handler's toes should be immediately in front of (but not touching) the dog's toes with this one slow step into position.**

The main idea behind this series of steps is to keep focus on the dog while backing away with leash tension.

During this initial step in front of the dog and throughout the subsequent steps of departure from your buddy, the left hand should remain in place next to your left hip and be the only hand grasping the leash. The same holds true even when we apply tension to the leash later in training. The purpose for holding the leash in this manner is to minimize the dog's focus on leash movement (thereby minimizing its importance in the dog's mind) while maximizing his focus on the command.

If your dog holds the *down* or *sit* posture, tell him, "Good Boy. Stay," at once. If your buddy rises from his obligated position as you move, instantly pivot back to *heel* and force him back to his proper place repeating the commands *down* or *sit* and *stay* as you pivot back to the front without delay.

In this first aspect of teaching *stay*, we must convey to the dog when he receives this directive that we are moving and he is not! It is critical to keep in mind here that the handler is to keep away from any extra commands or movements. We don't want to confuse our dog. The handler is leaving; the dog is staying. That is all we want to convey. Put no more distance between you and your canine partner than this one step until he is comfortable with the idea and can hold his posture for at least a half a minute or so. To release him from his *stay* obligation, simply return to the *heel* position beside him and give him your release command ("all done" finger snap, "free dog"—whatever you have chosen). Or you can give your dog a new command: *heel, walk, sit.* But it is very important that you establish a pattern of returning to the dog to release him from his *stay* obligation.

As soon as we have the first step of stay secure, we begin adding additional steps (one at a time) **with a little reverse leash tension to build up the opposition reflex.** This leash tension means that as we walk away, we gently pull him toward us, counting on him to remain in the *stay* position in spite of the pull. By teaching the dog to resist this tension originating from the handler as the handler retreats and by forcing him to dig into his *stay* position, we exponentially increase the strength of the dog's commitment to the command.

This leash tension originated by the handler is built up slowly over many training sessions with the left hand carried at the hip. Imagine the dog in his fixed position pulling the leash out of your left pocket. The left-hand grip should be soft at first, but firm enough to feel the leash slide through your hand. There should be enough tension in the leash, even in the initial *stay* exercises, to maintain a straight line between the dog and the handler. I typically apply the tension simultaneously with my departing movement, thereby connecting the command, the departure, and the tension all in one movement. With enough repetitions of this sequence (about twelve sessions in a week) over a long enough period of time (about three weeks), when you give your dog the command or signal to *stay*, he will not be able to keep himself from digging in while he watches you walk away. A reflexive response to lock up by command is what we want from this exercise and that is what you get with this approach.

A few notes are needed here about this reverse leash tension. As always, during the teaching phase of training when a dog breaks a command, replace him firmly and immediately move on with the exercise right where you left off. That means that when leash tension is being used to strengthen a *stay* position, as the handler departs and the dog gives in to the tension to follow the handler, once our buddy is physically returned to the original place and posture, the same amount of tension is immediately put back on the leash as the handler moves on with the exercise. Remember to quietly (no reprimands or reminders) replace the dog and then start over with a new command.

Be confident that your canine student is not confused about the purpose of this leash tension. With a soft, slow, one-step-at-a-time buildup, your dog will be clear early on that tension means dig in. (If this is hard to believe, please trust me and my ten thousand dogs' worth of experience.) I realize at first exposure to this technique that the reverse leash tension appears to be sending our canine partner a conflicting signal, but with this careful approach, it is not.

I don't want anyone to think that this buildup of the opposition reflex should be uncomfortable for the dog. Typically, we end up applying only enough tension to clearly see and feel our friend oppose the force and hold his spot. Also, the tension is usually only applied while the handler is moving away from the dog, full leash slack is returned as soon as the handler reaches his desired distance from the dog, whether we are talking about one step in front (toes to toes) or at the end of a ten-yard line (our backside to the dog) with a more experienced canine student.

Don't forget our goal: Your dog should remain in a hands-off *stay* in the midst of realistic distractions. With your dog in a sitting posture, we're shooting for one to two minutes. In a *down*, we are shooting for five to fifteen minutes. There is no better way that I have found to reach this goal than by using this reverse tension during the initial development of *stay*.

Making the transition from the teaching aspect of this command to its reinforcing should be a relatively comfortable process by this time for the reader. So I will cover only the specific considerations for *stay*. Expecting more from your dog and his *stay* obligation simply means more time in the posture, more distance from the handler, and more leash tension to resist.

Move the dog directly back to his original spot, not allowing him to touch you along the way.

During reinforcement, if your buddy moves from his designated spot (imagine that you left him on an X) or *significantly* changes his posture (from down to sit) without permission, the handler needs to replace him impressively, typically using the leash alone, to the exact spot in the original posture using no negative emotion. Do not allow your dog to creep, stretch, or roll off his X. Do not allow your friend to prematurely release himself from his obligation because you said, "Good boy," or gave a treat or returned to him. He must wait for your release. If he does not, the *stay* command is worthless. Every intelligent dog will find ample reasons to change the conditions of every *stay* so that he is once again in the mix of things. Keep in mind that your dog's staying put is one of the three most important elements of basic obedience so accept nothing less than 100 percent from your very capable canine companion.

At this point, the handler should be thinking of increasing distance and duration of the *stay* exercise through a series of one- or two-step moves, each move beginning with a command and/or signal and ending with praise (providing the dog holds) or repositioning (if he doesn't). As the training moves along, the handler adds more distance and time to each command until we end up with the desired result: a single command or signal holds the dog in place for a satisfactory time while the handler is a distance away.

Distractions, distractions, distractions! Proofing this command for real-life situations can only be second in importance to your dog's being able to come when called (our next and final formal command). And while you're conditioning your friend to hold his *stay* in the middle of temptations, develop an air as a handler of being pseudo busy. Convince your student that you can be in the training area working on other things (of no real importance) and still be an effective controller, capable of supplying positive and negative consequences connected to his behavior. However, do not actually get so involved during your dog's training that you forget about your friend's obligation. And remember, the greater the responsibility given to your dog, the more elaborate the reward for accomplishment. Never fail to recognize your faithful dog's effort, and your dog will never fail to try to please you.

As with all our obedience exercises, we don't need a perfect *stay* to be successful with training. We simply want to end up with a dependable, comfortable, don't-move response. You as a handler don't need to be flawless to be very effective. Your dog doesn't need to be anywhere near flawless to be well controlled. Your dog, you, and I—none of us were created flawless, thank goodness!

Exercise Ten: Come

We've now reached the top rung of our obedience ladder: come when called. It's the tenth step in our ten-step program because it demands the most from our dogs in the way of self-control. Therefore, our friend needs the buildup of energy control, handler deference, and distraction management the first nine rungs of the ladder give him in order to meet the necessary challenges and reach the tenth step in our program.

Here is why with the majority of dogs, the recall command (*come*) is the most demanding when considering self-control. We assume by the nature of the exercise (come back to us) our dog must be some distance away doing his own thing. I would also say that by the time the average dog reaches the age of sixteen to twenty weeks old, he has learned to appreciate his autonomy and has gained enough confidence (by virtue of maturing this far) that striking out on his own in pursuit of happiness (when the opportunity presents itself) can seem like a capital idea, oftentimes at the least convenient moment for the handler. And if you have a dog (young or old) who will bolt away from family and home when given the chance, it usually does not mean he's repulsed by his pack or den. Instead, he probably possesses a confident, curious, excitable personality and has learned that speed and opportunity equal stimulation and satisfaction (in other words, FUN).

When we assess the challenges of training a dog to come when called, we must factor into the assessment these realities: the dog is out of our reach; he is at least a little stimulated; he is faster than we are (even if he only has three legs); and even if he has only followed through with this *come* idea once before, our good buddy knows that some kind of control or confinement is usually waiting for him when he gets to us. So, in essence, when we command our dog to come, we're asking him to give up his cherished autonomy and give up his free world of abundant stimulation for some form of restriction when he *knows* we can't possibly catch him if he doesn't want us to! The next time you see a dog run to his handler when called and sit in front waiting for instruction, think to yourself, "WOW. That's self-control."

There are reasons we need nine steps of drive control, handler deference, and distraction management under the dog's belt before we tackle this command.

I used to find it irritating early in my career when a new client, after hearing my explanation of the basic obedience process, would tell me he didn't need any of that staying or heeling malarkey. He just wanted his dog to come! Now, years and many gray hairs later, I genuinely laugh out loud at a naïve client like that and then present him with this analogy. Imagine coaching a young teenager to be an Olympic high platform diver. Rather than start out on the side of the pool working on foot placement and basic water entry techniques, you decide as the teenager's coach that you will skip the fundamentals along the poolside. In addition, you decide that springboard training has nothing to offer your student. For that matter, it's a waste of time to dive from the lower platform when it is the high dive you're really after. It doesn't take Olympic diving experience to quickly realize that this coach has his student on the fast track to failure with this training approach.

So it is with the recall exercise. A handler is asking for frustration and failure if he doesn't thoroughly prepare his dog for this high platform event. Having a dog prepared to look through distractions and focus on his handler is a definite must for this exercise. And having a dog in control of his energy is a must before you begin this exercise. Assuming you began reading this book somewhere near the front and assuming that you have worked with your dog with at least limited success through the first nine training exercises, then you and your dog are ready for the "big dive."

For starters, I want every handler to look at the recall exercise as a position obligation for the dog (sit in front looking at the handler). This will keep everyone (handlers and dogs) zeroed in on what's really important: a controlled, focused dog within easy reach of his handler.

I teach *come* with no real distance between the dog and me at first. I begin with the dog's name (to get his attention) because up to this point, he's just been hanging out with me on leash. I immediately follow the dog's name with the designated command (*come*) or signal for his new obligation.

I then place him in a sitting position directly in front of me, using my leash in the left hand, directing his head toward my belt buckle. At the same time, I use my right hand over his spine gripping his loin to place his rump on the floor in one fluid motion.

Be sure and give the come command or signal on a loose leash, using the leash only for placement.

107

As soon as I have him in this sitting position looking up at me, I instantly reward him with praise and/or food. Telling your dog to sit during the placement process is really not necessary, but it doesn't hurt anything as long as there is a quiet pause after placement before the *come* command is given. We want the emphasis of this exercise to rest on the command or signal to come, not to sit.

Before you deliver any praise, make sure your canine friend is sitting freely (no leash tension or grip on the loin) and looking up at you while you're standing erect. We want to make a clear association between the dog's sitting closely in front of the handler with his attention focused on the handler (who is standing quietly upright) and the appropriate signal and/or command. That's when our buddy receives his reward—after he fulfills his new obligation.

As you did in all the other preceding placement commands, don't hurry your dog out of this position once you get him there. Definitely don't allow your dog to release himself. Remember, we're teaching our dog that *come* means to sit in front focused on the handler until the dog is released. During the teaching aspect of this command, like with the previous exercises, we only expect a very brief hold on the dog's part at first, but we need to insist on a little commitment even the first time we place him.

When I release the dog from these early recall exercises, I don't allow him to go far. I will continue to hold the leash after I tell him "all done" because I intend simply to pivot away from the dog after a brief moment and repeat the command, the placement, and the praise. Each time I practice this recall exercise, I'll run through this series of repetitions. Our goal is to drive home during teaching exactly where *come* is, just as we did with the other placement commands. When we get to the reinforcement aspect of this training, we will accept nothing less.

I typically don't muddy the waters around this command by calling the dog from a *stay* position until the dog shows me, while working with the *come* command, that I can pivot in any direction I want to any degree and back away (with the dog on leash and leash in hand) as far as I want, and he will work to sit in front of me. The dog's response doesn't have to be exact before I call him from a *stay* (with a little distance), but the dog needs to be comfortable with his new *come* obligation before I complicate it with *stay*.

Since dogs seem to tend to think in mental images, with enough repetitions of sit placement in front of the handler in association with the command *come*, the command or signal given prior to placement will eventually conjure up in our friend's mind the idea that he's supposed to sit in front of the handler. This association between signal and position and reward is what the teaching phase of training is all about for all formal commands. And you know the teaching is finished when you give the command and your dog is already working into correct posture or position before you have had a chance to place him.

There are a few things to keep in mind when you begin teaching your dog to come from a *stay* position. First of all, your buddy may be reluctant to break the *stay* command in order to follow the *come* command. After all, we did drive home the idea of not breaking the stay position until we as handlers return to the spot and release the dog. This idea was absolutely necessary during *stay* training to bring about a solid, dependable response. So now when we teach *come* from a *stay*, we should be easy with our buddy and encourage him to move towards our front with some very light leash tugs (not tension and pulling which would resemble reverse tension for developing the opposition reflex) and some light, encouraging words like "Good girl" (be careful not to lavish your student with praise until she is in the proper sit-in-front position). Try to avoid repeating the command or signal during this encouragement. We still want to end up with a complete response from a single directive. This period of reluctance to break a *stay* to satisfy *come* won't last very long at all. Just be positive and patient and your dog will catch on quickly.

This sticky wicket of breaking the *stay* to satisfy *come* is the primary reason I teach the recall position (sitting in front of the handler) first, so as not to unnecessarily stress or confuse my students. Along this same line of thinking, make sure your leash is loosely held in the left hand (left hand next to left hip) no differently than you would with the stay exercise after you have applied the reverse tension for opposition development.

We don't want the dog conflicted on the command *come*. We want him to be able to comfortably concentrate on this new command or signal and the obligation that goes with it.

By keeping your leash loose and your body still when you call your dog from a stay, you're allowing him to zero in on the exact signal or command you want him to respond to. If you're not careful, you might inadvertently teach your friend that a leash shake, a thigh pat, or stepping backward are all part of this command. A dog needs very simple signals.

Once you have developed a smooth, single directive response to *come* from a *stay* position (both sit and down) while standing still, add backing away from the dog, leash in hand, and changing directions (always leading with your backside). By traveling backward with direction changes, we're teaching the dog to focus on the handler's front, honing in on the recall position in other words. We're also helping the dog to develop concentration stamina over distance which is just what we need from him on a real off-leash recall outside. I don't care how far or how fast you back away from your dog.

Your dog's job is to pursue your belt buckle on a loose leash and sit when he gets there.

When you're teaching this part of the recall exercise, back away slowly at first and don't travel too far. Use only light leash checks (tugs) to keep your student focused on your front. But as teaching turns into reinforcement (in only a matter of days), the distance you back up can be greatly increased. Your speed should vary from very fast to very slow as you travel this distance. You should also include some challenging direction changes in this moving exercise. And since the training has shifted into the reinforcing phase, our leash checks (when needed) are considerably more important.

Create real obstacle courses for your dog to come through.

At this stage of recall development, a handler should feel free to administer negative leash and collar consequences for the following: failure to respond to the first command, failure to come all the way into recall position, failure to sit when the dog gets into position, or failure to pursue the handler's front when practicing recall in motion. Of course, all of these responsibilities are loose-leash obligations for the dog. Remember, if the negative consequence becomes more potent for failure, then the positive consequences need to be more potent for success. In this phase of training, we do expect more from the dog so the consequences should be considerable. Such is the nature of reinforcement.

Using the Long Line

Before I take this recall exercise into true distraction proofing, I like to practice for a number of days with the dog on a long line. Depending on the particulars of a handler/dog relationship, I usually suggest a length of line from twenty-five to fifty feet. Again, handling adeptness, training environment conditions, and the dog's personality will determine what length of line is best suited for any given situation.

Along with practicing *come* on a long line, I will also be reinforcing *stay* (both in the sit and down postures) from a greater distance and introducing *down* at a distance. With all these ideas, once I've connected the line to the collar and uncoiled its length on the ground, I only work with the amount of line I need at the time, ignoring the rest. As the dog's proficiency in each exercise improves, I gradually increase my distance from my student, eventually working out to the end of the long line. Begin as close to the dog as needed and then work out.

This long line practice puts real distance between the dog and the handler for the first time in the context of formal command response. For the dog, this means the first opportunity to test his misperceived autonomous options and to blow off his handler's formal commands. In this stage of training, we actually want our students to test the water over and over again. We want our students to exercise what appears to them to be their independent option of refusing our commands. With enough failed attempts on the dog's part, his independence doesn't seem so real anymore and thoughts of putting his spin on our command really don't come to the surface much.

In order to foster this feeling of autonomy in your dog, you must handle the long line smartly. Think of stealthy management when utilizing a long line or your leash for that matter. The less the dog thinks about the leash or long line, the less it matters to him, on or off. So if we're careful and manage the long line with the same loose concern, the same minimal hand movements as we've practiced with the leash, we're actually laying the foundation for off-leash control. With this in mind, I typically uncoil my ten-meter line before I clip it to my dog's collar and simply let him drag it around. Sometimes I will hold on to the end of the line if I am dealing with a new, challenging student.

When the dog walks on the line or when the line gets wrapped up around a bush or a chair leg or when the line is dragged through mud or water, think "So what?!" This long-line work is the indispensable bridge between hands-on and hands-off control over your dog.

Keep in mind that the more a dog wears his long line or leash (loose in hand or dragging around) the more it becomes a part of his body, a tail on the front end. Once a dog is completely accustomed to dragging around a long line, his behavior normalizes. So the behavior we're shaping with the long line is eventually the same behavior we will get with the long line off.

There are a few things to consider when preparing for long-line practice. First of all, there is no way around the fact that the longer the leash or line is, the more awkward it will be to deal with. So always accomplish as much as you can with your shorter training leash in order to minimize the amount of work you'll have to do on the clumsy longer line. That's why with the recall exercise, I suggest a lot of practice with the backward motion and direction change during the close-in shorter leash work. This simulates distance and travel for the dog while still affording the handler the convenience of a shorter training leash for control.

Secondly, corrections are much more difficult to deliver with a long line. Excess slack will accumulate between the dog and the handler. The line will become wrapped around the dog's legs, people's legs, bushes, and furniture. Also, given the various amounts of elasticity in the long lines we use, despite our best efforts, the line correction will be somewhat spongy or anemic compared to our leash correction. These difficulties plague all handlers, even professionals, when working with the long line. I will give you a few tips that will be helpful in managing these challenges.

Tip one: Make a habit of throwing excess slack between the handler and the dog behind you when you pick up the long line to use. Let the excess fall on the ground. Only hold a single strand of line in your hand, no loops or bundles.

Tip two: Casually follow the line as your dog drags it around, and, as stealthily as you can, take care of tangles and wraps before they become problematic. Use your foot to move the long line out from under the door. While your dog is engrossed in a smell, unwrap the line from around the bush. As your buddy trots along, smoothly grab the line and unwind his leg though the dog will usually take care of that himself. The long line between the dog's legs or under the belly is fine. The long line wrapped around the legs or neck is not fine.

Long lines are awkward but indispensable when developing hands-off control.

To be most effective in long-line work, the key is stealth. We don't want the dog thinking any more about this line than he absolutely has to, even when we are untangling, dealing with slack, or preparing for corrections. We need our dog to feel as off leash as possible, so allow the line to drag and only refer to it when you absolutely have to.

Tip three: When a long line check is needed, step on the line first before you pick it up. This stops the dog in his tracks and allows the handler to gain a secure grip instantly.

If the line in use is slight in diameter, it may be necessary to wrap it around your hand or wear a glove to ensure a good grip or prevent chafing. Assuming you have picked up the leash, thrown the excess slack behind you on the ground, and secured a grip, you are now ready for the line check (correction).

Depending greatly on the size, strength, and energy level of the dog in training, the line tug could be administered with one hand, two hands, or two hands and a backward step. The goal is always the same. We want a crisp, attention-grabbing jolt that halts undesirable behavior. If the long line happens to be wrapped around one of your dog's limbs at the moment he needs a correction, you must take the time to quickly unwrap and then follow through with the intended correction. If the line is simply between the legs or underneath the dog, lower the line or the angle of the tug so as not to raise the dog off the ground, but follow through with the correction. Don't worry about adjusting the line in this case.

I will tell you again, long-line work is awkward but so necessary! Do as much as you can on the regular training leash. There is no need to hurry to the long line. And maybe, after doing thorough foundation work, you might find that your ace canine student doesn't need much work in this area after all.

Now comes the fun part: recall practice in, around, and over distractions. This is always where the rubber meets the road, so don't hold back when setting up these proofing exercises. As always, build the intensity of the distractions gradually, but don't fool around. Make sure you can call your dog over an open box of pizza. See to it that your partner has no trouble coming around another handler and dog to get to your front and sit. And if he does run into a snag and is unable to leave the treed squirrel or the kids playing ball, don't hesitate to use that leash or long line. That is what they are for. Remember when using the long line (hands on or hands off), we expect the same immediate and complete follow-through from the *come* command that we did back when we were standing directly in front of the dog with the short leash in hand. With all of our training, what we expect from our four-legged friend with leash in hand, we will eventually expect with the leash off!

Do not let up until your recall is 100 percent.

In closing, be mindful of the clock when training your friend. Fifteen to thirty minutes should be enough time to work on everything from handling manners through hands-off recall on a long line. We never want to train beyond our dog's capacity to concentrate.

Enjoy working with your dog and he'll enjoy working with you. He is a family member after all, not a soldier. Also, make natural dog time a regular part of his life. All of our canine friends need some time just to be animals. Running, barking, jumping, chewing, and smelling are all essential activities for a healthy dog. And a healthy, happy, controlled dog is a joy to live with!

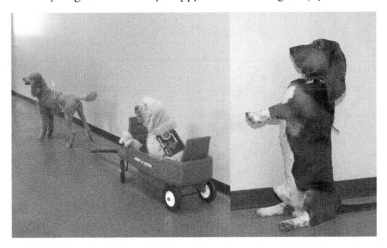

Keep training fun!

Frequently Asked Questions

A door is what a dog is perpetually on the wrong side of.
—Ogden Nash, The Private Dining Room (1953)

At the training center, we get a lot of questions every day. Some of these questions have answers too complex for this book. I will deal with a good many of these problems in later volumes. In the meantime, here are some guidelines that I hope will help.

Aggression

My dog seems to be aggressive without provocation toward other dogs and some people. Why, even with training, does he persist in being distracted?

The most serious problem behavior a dog owner can face is aggression. Whether you are talking about injury, liability, or emotional upset, a hostile canine personality must be dealt with expeditiously. It is a rare day indeed when I lock up the training center door at the close of business without having wrestled with a couple of aggressive dogs.

Because aggression is such a prevalent and complex question, volume 2 in this series will take up the aggression problem in depth. However, in this book, let me say that I think the best way for an owner to understand aggressive potential in his or her pet is to view the behavior as an aspect of character or personality the same way we might with a human being who tends to be hot tempered or fierce. I use the metaphor of facets on a diamond to illustrate for my clients the essence of this tendency in many dogs. A dog can display several types of aggression, and, like facets on a diamond, these aspects of personality cannot be removed from the animal. With effective training, however, they can be pushed out of sight so that eventually, the dog's tendency toward aggression is no longer visible.

Spoiling

I have heard that you can spoil your dog with too much praise or ruin your dog with too much discipline. I love my dog, but want her to behave. On the other hand, I don't want to break her playful spirit. How do I draw the line between spoiling my dog and over-disciplining her?

I have seen that there's really no such thing as too much attention or affection for your dog. As long as the relationship between dog and owner is balanced, meaning the owner is clearly in charge and the dog is content in deferring to his handler, no harm will come from an abundance of loving attention.

I want to repeat: The owner must be the absolute authority in a healthy relationship. If a dog sneaks onto the bed after his handler falls asleep (knowing very well that he's going against his handler's wishes) or harasses his owner by barking, whining, jumping, and pawing until the master placates him or bullies his way onto the couch to lick the dessert plate, the dog is in charge and the relationship is out of balance.

The truth of the matter is that there is nothing inherently wrong with a dog sleeping in bed with his owners or being carried around by his master or sitting on the couch or finishing the big dog's dessert just as long as the big dog (the handler) approves of and initiates the plan.

Along these same lines, confusion over the differences between soothing and rewarding versus coddling and pampering often hampers positive, effective dog training. Let's say a handler and his dog are walking down the sidewalk when the dog spooks at a strange-looking garbage can. It would be detrimental to the dog's confidence to switch sides of the street at that moment to continue the walk. Likewise, to stop at the garbage can and console the dog, trying to coax him past, only attributes more importance and anxiety to an object or situation that warrants little or none.

The proper approach to this dilemma is to force the dog to remain on course (using light leash and collar tugs) without using legitimate correction or dragging. Try not to deviate from the original walking plan at all. Do not acknowledge the garbage can at all. Do not address the dog's anxiety except to reassure him that he is walking or heeling all right and that you are calm and pleased with his efforts. In other words, buck up. Calm the dog with your calmness. Bolster his confidence with your confidence. Keep him focused by remaining focused, and try to have fun so your dog will have fun.

Just like with a parent and child, a handler's emotional state bleeds directly over the dog. A handler's mind-set eventually becomes the dog's

mind-set. A handler and dog work as a team. The handler is the captain and sets a standard for the team.

The opposite of coddling is not necessarily a good thing either. In the case of a shy or defensive dog who tries to hide from or run off certain visitors, forcing the visitor or the dog to make friends is just as bad as reassuring the dog that her hiding or growling is okay by lavishing sweet talk on her and caressing her. With either of these approaches, the dog's anxiety over visitors generally grows. Instead, your cheerful calmness will set the tone that the dog will adopt.

During the years 2006 and 2007, I was involved in the city of Louisville, Kentucky's, heated debate over a new dangerous dog ordinance. I was representing the Louisville Kennel Club as a behavioral consultant. At one of the meetings, I was asked a very pertinent question about dog ownership.

I was asked what can compel an overly empathetic and permissive dog owner to become a responsible disciplinarian. My response to this seemingly complex question was rather short. The only catalyst I've witnessed in two and half decades of professional training potent enough to bring about this kind of remarkable change is the immediate negative consequence of the permissive dog owner's dog's repugnant behavior.

The negative consequences usually need to be substantial like personal injury, real property damage, a lawsuit, or a hefty fine in order to force action in the passive owner.

I worked with some of the most frustrating cases over the years, listening to the owners excuse away their dog's offensive behavior as if it were naturally someone else's fault. The lady at the park said that her rowdy Labrador ran across the walkway and body slammed a four-year-old child because he thought the girl was inviting him to wrestle while she was trying to jump rope. Uncle Charlie said that his sweet, female Jack Russell bit the mailman on the leg because he was walking entirely too fast back to his truck. My sister said her hound-mix snatched the cake off my plate because I said "sweet" and her dog heard "treat" and assumed I must be eating his dessert. This is my all-time favorite justification: Our cocker spaniel sneaked into our bedroom, rooted through our closet, and chewed to smithereens a new pair of boots because she thought it was her toy.

During most of this excuse-making, the majority of pet owners are still trying to sell themselves on their dog's innocence, hoping to avoid the ugly (their perception, not mine) responsibility of discipline. I think it's a shame that so many pet owners feel that you must either be a nurturer or a disciplinarian. In truth, the very best dog handlers are an equal blend of both, no different from the very best parents.

There is absolutely no reason why a dog owner can't lavish his pet with praise and affection before or after a sharp, effective correction for unacceptable behavior. In fact, at my training center, this balanced approach to dog handling represents the core of our highly successful training philosophy.

I firmly believe that if a handler views a disciplinary action as a mechanical leash and collar (not emotional) consequence inextricably connected to a behavior, so will the dog. I operate this principle with my own dog, going as far as purposefully playing with or soothing my buddy before and after a difficult learning experience. We constantly preach "no negative emotion" at the training center. By minimizing reprimands and eliminating hostile emotional displays during leash and collar corrections, a handler can expedite positive recovery from discipline even with the most sensitive dog. A good handler should not take his dog's challenge or wrong action personally. The only way even the most intelligent dog can learn where his parameters are is to test them. Elucidating with words alone the differences between right and wrong action barely works with children and doesn't work at all with animals.

The flip side of this same relationship coin is nurturing. Here, genuine positive emotion should be utilized to soothe or stimulate the pet in training. **The key word in this bit of advice is *genuine*.** If a handler allows himself to get worked up over a dog's mistakes and administers an emotional correction, typically the resulting positive change in the dog's behavior is followed only by anemic praise. This pattern of emotional correction and weak reward will most certainly develop a tendency towards an overall negative relationship between handler and dog. Reverse this pattern (sharp, mechanical correction with weak emotion followed by personal, genuine praise) and the opposite will always be true: an overall positive relationship between the owner and his best friend.

A tip for novice handlers especially, learning how to minimize discipline and maximize the nurturing aspects of their owner-dog relationship: Closely observe and learn to recognize a deteriorating situation in regard to the dog's behavior. When I am responsible for an untrained dog's behavior, I consider myself "on the clock," meaning that I keep the dog in visual contact with leash and collar at the ready. And just as soon as I recognize a behavioral slide in the wrong direction, I step into leash action without a warning. With this approach, a minimal correction is all that I will need to redirect the dog's focus down a positive path where praise lies in store.

When I'm off the clock, I put my dog in his comfortable, safe area. Of course, as training proceeds, your pet should require less and less concentrated supervision. Being slow to recognize or act on a wrong behavior means our pet will be more deeply committed to this unacceptable maneuver and thus require more substantial discipline in order to redirect his focus. Of course, this amounts to more negativity overall and more recovery time from the learning experience.

Our motto at the training center is this: **Act early, act sharply, thereby minimizing any residual negativity associated with the learning experience.** Remember, the faster you get through the correction, the faster you get the praise. Utilizing warnings rather than action or being slow to commit to discipline only escalates the inevitable confrontation.

By all means, concentrate on nurturing, but don't be afraid to administer a healthy dose of discipline when called for. By following this advice, you're guaranteed to end up in a rewarding and loving relationship with your dog.

To illustrate in human terms the thrust of this motto, I'll tell a story about my son Zachary and a freshly painted wall. Zachary, who was about six at the time, was helping (mostly talking to me) while I painted a large wall in one of our center's training rooms. We had a long conversation during this task about how long it would take for all the paint to dry. I could tell my estimations on drying time didn't quite satisfy Zachary's six-year-old curiosity. So when the painting was done and I was walking out of the room to clean the brushes, I gave Zachary very clear instructions to leave the newly painted walls alone.

Knowing my son the way I do, walking past him, I saw in his eyes the overwhelming urge to test my theory on the drying time. No sooner than I had passed through the doorway, I looked back to see Zack, hands in pockets, moving directly toward the large wall. Without hesitation, I set my tools on the floor and made a beeline for my son.

I immediately picked him up and sat him on a chair, giving instructions to remain on that chair until I returned. Before I left, I did explain to Zachary the reasoning behind my actions (something, unfortunately, dogs miss out on). The directive to leave the wall alone was ignored the moment Zachary began to gravitate toward it. There was no need for me to wait for any further proof that he was on his way to investigate the paint. And naturally, since Zachary would not have been able to satisfy his inquisitive, impatient mind simply by looking at the paint, touching the wall would have been the necessary follow-up. Returning to Zachary after cleaning the brushes, I gave him a hug and hold him he was a good fella for waiting in the chair.

By taking immediate, decisive action, I was able to defuse the situation before any real damage occurred while demonstrating to my young son that I mean what I say and that there are consequences for his actions. All this was accomplished with almost no negativity and without the need to nag or ride herd, thereby preserving a positive atmosphere for learning.

121

Etiquette in Public Places

My border collie is perfectly trained. My problem is other people and their dogs. Sometimes we go out in public like the park or the pet store or the vet, and invariably, a rowdy dog joins us. The dog is a distraction at best and a danger at worst. What should I tell the owner of the dog when the owner (finally) catches her dog and tells me that her dog was "only playing"?

This is really an annoying problem. I strongly believe that all dog owners out in public places with their canine companions need to abide by some basic rules of etiquette. Like you, when I take my dog out in public, I want to spend time with him, not someone else's dog. I plan on my dog interacting with my family not with other dogs. No matter how nice other dogs are—and in my work, I see many nice dogs every day—good social manners dictate that I should be the one who invites another dog to join us. I should be afforded the same freedoms of choice that I give you and your dog when we meet in a public place. Do I want the challenge of controlling high energy or tension in my companion because you and/or your dog come within contact distance? Do I have to defend myself and my family (including the four-legged members) against your dog's enthusiastic, often offensive, feet and mouth? Social etiquette suggests that I can opt out of those potential scenarios by simply saying no and that this should not hurt the imposing dog owner's feelings.

Sometimes my dog and I enjoy interacting with others; sometimes we don't. And that should be okay. Occasionally, I meet dogs out in public that aren't nearly as friendly as their owners say they are, and I would rather not deal with them at all. Frequently, I encounter dogs in public places that aren't as tidy as one might like, and I would just as soon they keep their pungent coating to themselves.

When dogs are in control, the owners are just along for the ride and excuse away rude behavior as natural. ("That's just what dogs do." "He just wants to visit." "Don't be afraid; he's friendly." "He just wants to see what your daughter is eating." "He's just trying to play.") My response is always the same in these situations: I don't care what your dog wants or what he's trying to do or what you think is natural. To me, your dog is disturbing. Take control of your dog, and ask permission or wait for an invitation.

When you meet up with a dog on public ground, whether he is on a leash with an owner or off leash with an owner, or maybe without an owner, you must acknowledge a certain unpredictability in his behavior simply because he is an animal. That's not necessarily a good fact or a bad fact. It's just a fact. This unpredictability combined with the unpredictability of a strange person's reaction (like swatting at your tail-wagging dog as he approaches for a sniff) can lead to a potentially volatile situation.

My exposure to this kind of situation is greatly amplified compared to the ordinary pet owner because I train dogs for a living. I meet an average of two new dogs with their owners every working day and have for over two and a half decades. Routinely, I must block the advance of a new client's bristling, growling dog (owner in tow) with a chair, appointment book, or my body to prevent an unpleasant contact with another dog or person only to hear the new client cry out with embarrassment that his dog has never behaved like that before. Whether the client's claim of unexpected behavior is true or not is actually immaterial. The outcome would have been the same. And often, an innocent passerby finds out in the heat of the moment that the offensive dog's owner had no plan to manage the situation.

I hear countless stories of dogs being approached by friendly people and, for some unexplained reason, snapping at some who attempt to touch while accepting others passively. More times than I can recall, I've sat across from a new client with his dog on a leash during a temperament evaluation and have had to repeatedly remove the dog from my lap and insist that the owner keep him restrained while we talk.

"My dog seems to like you; he bit the last person he climbed on," the owner says.

This is not an exaggerated example of the response I occasionally receive when asking some clients to rein their dogs in. I don't know if they think maybe some people are immune to dog bites or maybe that this particular visitor might be one of the lucky ones who walks away intact or if maybe this kind of dog owner is simply sadistic. The truth is this: As with many canine behaviors, the untrained owner may be unable or unwilling to deal with the problem or too embarrassed to acknowledge that there is a problem at all so they simply hope for the best. The moral of this story is to be cautious around unfamiliar dogs and be even more cautious around unfamiliar people.

An aspect of dog-to-dog visits at the park that most people don't consider until it's too late is the possible transmission of parasites such as fleas and worms and the possibility of your dog's contracting a virus from another dog. A comparable human encounter to dogs' sniffing noses and necking over one another would be two strangers haphazardly meeting at the ball field and immediately falling into an embrace with an open-mouth kiss. Now I don't know about you, but that would be way too risky for me regardless of how neat and clean that stranger might appear to be. So if I meet you out on a dog walk, don't be offended if I prevent our dogs from kissing.

Leash laws are good! You shouldn't have to trust my off-leash control of my dog when you are in a public place.

If your dog were your child, would you let one of them impose on someone else's picnic? Would you permit your child to aggressively approach someone else's child? The same manners we demand for our children should be the ones we insist on for our dogs.

Also, clean up after your friend. Be a good citizen. You would not think of leaving your child's diapers around a public place. But strangely, people don't think about their dogs' elimination in this way. That's because when dogs urinate or defecate it is "natural." As I said before, have a place on your property that your dog knows is the place for defecation and urination. Do not permit your dog to hike his leg wherever he wishes. Understand his digestive tract well enough to know that food spends approximately eight hours in your dog's body before defecation. Plan your time in public places with your dog. Let me say again that a responsible pet owner should be ready at all times to clean up if accidents happen.

Dog parks frighten me. I know they work for many owners and their pets, but they have the potential to be lethal. Rarely have I spent long in a dog park without watching at least one fight break out as dogs jockey for dominance. In addition, there is the ever-present danger of dogs infecting other dogs. However, if you are a dog park advocate, petition for a space that is just for dogs, enclosed with a space for large dogs separate from a space for smaller dogs. Be sure your dog park has an adequate water supply and consider carrying your dog's water with you along with a traveling bowl. Many dog parks now have gates that are controlled by magnetic keys. To get in, the dog owner pays a fee and must show proof of the dog's inoculations. Take every precaution possible when dealing with multiple strange dogs.

Training and equipment mean freedom for you and your dog. Many people look at a slip collar and a leash as a way of restricting a dog. Instead, using training tools effectively is a way of liberating you and your dog. And the process of teaching your dog and watching your dog learn is a process that binds the two of you closer than you might have ever hoped. People who tell me that their dog can read their minds (while the dog is, at that moment, struggling against their restraint) always strike me as funny. If the dog could *really* read your mind, I want to say, he would know you are plenty tired of pulling at that leash.

But with training, there is a much closer harmony between you and your dog. Your dog will come to know, with your slightest gesture, what you are asking. And you will come to know your dog better too.

Often, in dealing with public manners, I have to talk to dog owners about muzzles. Muzzles keep dogs from biting. You might think that your Great Dane doesn't need a muzzle because he doesn't bite. In fact, your Great

Dane is the gentlest dog you have ever known. I can appreciate your point of view.

But in my experience, even the gentlest animal is still an animal. There is always a chance for unpredictable behavior. And when your dog is at the vet or at the groomer, a place where strangers routinely handle your dog in intimate and unfamiliar ways, it is possible that your gentle dog might snap or even bite.

Do not put the professionals who care for your dog in uncomfortable positions. If your dog is larger than a Yorkie, as a matter of courtesy, ask that your dog be muzzled during treatment. Think of how disconcerting it is for a vet to be ready to inoculate a dog while the owner says that he will try to hold the dog's head. Responsible dog owners take responsibility for their dogs.

In Europe, notably France and Germany, dogs are permitted in restaurants and dogs behave. It would be wonderful if here, in the United States, dogs were more welcome in public places. It is, sadly, clear why they are not. However, do your part to be an ambassador for dogs. In every public situation, ask yourself if your dog is a model citizen, and if not, take appropriate steps. Remember that your dog will only be as good a citizen as you are.

Excessive Barking

We are at our wits' end. We have a large fenced-in yard that opens by dog door into a climate-controlled garage. Our two beagles spend the night outside. As soon as the sun begins to come up, they begin barking. One of our nice neighbors has had to call. What can we do to train our dogs not to bark?

Dogs should be in their secure area when the owner is not present, and that does not necessarily include a yard. Put a crate in your climate-controlled garage, and invite your beagles each into their crates for the night. You will find that the barking problem will stop. Another possible solution might be the use of a bark-diminishing collar during the critical time.

Housebreaking

Help! My dog is five months old and still isn't housebroken. How do you housebreak your dog?

Every other call that rings into the training center is about the all-stressing elimination routine. Usually by the time an owner calls us, he or she is neck-deep in frustration and willing to try anything, which makes straightforward advice almost fun.

Housebreaking any dog, regardless of breed, age, or background, boils down to four responsibilities for the owner: **proper confinement, supervision with leash attached, relief schedule, and regulated access to food and water.**

There are a few things to discuss before we walk through the process. First of all, we must assume that our pet slated for housebreaking is in good physical condition and capable of holding an elimination for at least several hours. Dogs typically not capable of this control are puppies younger than sixteen weeks, senior canines who have become incontinent, and dogs suffering from urinary tract infections or digestive tract problems.

Assuming our pet is physically up to the task, the first thing we square away is proper indoor confinement. In respect to housebreaking, we refer to confinement as an escape-proof area small enough to compel a dog to keep clean, usually a generous bed size. Our hope is that this area is small enough to discourage the pet from soiling it for fear of stepping in his mess. For this reason, a room in the house of any size is generally too large to be effective. The available products already on the market are usually best, such as wire cages and plastic crates. The vast majority of dogs we deal with usually respond favorably to these conditions once they have been properly introduced to them.

Remember, an owner should not use this confinement as punishment or time-out quarters. We want this cage or crate to represent pleasant personal space for safekeeping. There should be no food or water left with a dog when he is confined like this. Bedding in the crate or cage is fine as long as our canine avoids soiling it (absorbent surfaces allow a mess to be more tolerable to the dog) or destroying it (out of frustration or for entertainment).

Leaving some form of appropriate chewing item with the dog is a plus. Using this approach to confinement, we are counting on our friend's inherent tendency to keep his bed clean. Unfortunately, a small percentage of dogs don't seem to care. In fact, a few of our friends appear to gain a little satisfaction or stress relief from a beautifully messed bed. If you happen to be one of the lucky owners who have come across a new family member of this nature, you will have no choice but to reduce the confinement area to the dog's body space (only temporarily) to reduce the freedom of comfortable elimination postures.

The bed-sized cage or crate can be sized down in these situations by utilizing indestructible partitions available commercially or homemade partitions. Of course, for most of us owners, the goal is to gradually work the dog into larger portions of the house which will happen in time.

Proper supervision, our second all-important responsibility, requires two critical considerations: a designated handler or handlers along with a collar and leash attached to the canine (for quick action). **To be successful at housebreaking, a dog *must* be within visual contact of a designated handler *100 percent* of the time he is outside of his confinement while in the house.**

Assuming our friend is dragging his leash about, when a handler witnesses a dog attempting to eliminate or in the process of eliminating, he must immediately grab the leash supplying moderate tugs to create distraction along with a sense of negativity over the behavior and whisk the dog outside to the appropriate bathroom spot. Our friend should be taken outside even if he has completed the elimination inside so that the handler can convey a positive feel for the proper place.

Given the propensity for accidents in the house during this teaching process, it would behoove the owner to restrict his pet (out of confinement) to the floor which is easiest to clean. In regard to the messes in the house, the moderate tugs on the leash at the time of action are the only corrections needed. No old-school rubbing his nose in the filth or chastising is necessary; simply and quietly clean the floor if warranted. Then pleasantly move on to normal activities. There should be no excuses for not catching the dog in the act; therefore, no eliminations should now happen in the house without immediate negative consequences. Neglect of this responsibility is the most common reason the average pet owner fails at housebreaking.

Also, don't allow your buddy to chew on the leash as he drags it around. It is your valuable property, not your dog's. (Use standard leash and collar corrections if he tries.)

There is nothing wrong with a designated handler taking a break from his or her supervision duties any time a break is desired, even if it's only for three minutes while the person brushes his or her teeth. Simply put the dog in the confinement space and release your friend when supervision seems doable again. The more a confinement space is utilized for short periods, the less there will be distaste associated with it.

Frequent use of a cage or crate is a good thing to keep in mind when first setting it up in the house. I'm going to pass on a valuable piece of advice, realized from personally working with thousands of families and their housebreaking woes: Don't allow yourself to feel guilty over frequent confinement; acting on such guilt will overcome your good work. Remember, this confinement is very temporary.

Our third responsibility of relief schedule can vary quite a bit from case to case. However, there are seven key relief opportunities necessary for housebreaking success: 1. When you rise in the morning, do not run from your bed to the crate. Take your time and get ready; this will develop patience in your dog; 2. after a period of play; 3. following a substantial nap; 4. just before the last person leaves the house; 5. just after the first person arrives home; 6. immediately after the dog eats or drinks a considerable amount; 7. right before the last handler retires for the night.

Although these seven relief periods represent the most important opportunities for elimination, they by no means need to be the only times a dog has a chance. I would caution the reader here not to establish an elimination routine that cannot be adhered to in the future. That is, taking a week's worth of vacation from work so that you can take your new puppy out to use the bathroom every hour (knowing very well that you can only maintain this schedule a week) only leads to false expectations in the dog and failure to housebreak. Stick to a routine that is workable for both family and dog so that the routine can become the normal way the family operates.

Regulating access to food and water is our final and easiest responsibility in regards to housebreaking. Among professionals, there are two schools of thought on feeding arrangements for dogs: One is free feeding (food available all the time) where the pet is allowed to regulate how much and how often he eats. The other is an owner-governed eating schedule.

A distinct minority of clients passing through our training center allow their pets to free feed. Surprisingly, most of the dogs we see on this system seem to maintain good body weight. However, free feeding can interfere with housebreaking by allowing the dog to eat frequently or excessively, thereby stimulating his system to eliminate frequently or excessively (not in all cases, but in many).

I know this to be true because in countless problem housebreaking situations, the only thing we recommend a family adjust is the eating arrangement because all else seems to be in order. When the eating arrangement changes, the problem disappears.

For this reason, we try to set all of our house-training candidates on a one- to two-meal-a-day plan. Regulating intake seems to help regulate output. As for my personal dogs (good health and moderate activity assumed) a normal twenty-four hour ration is divided into three meals for a pup up to three months old, then two meals for one up to five months old. From that point on, I feed one meal a day.

The quality of the food given to your dog should also be seriously considered when discussing housebreaking and overall health. Cheaper dog foods on the market are comprised of fillers including a high percentage of grain that our pets don't process very well. This translates into the dog consuming a large percentage of food that they can't assimilate very well, which leads to more stool and poorer health. Get suggestions from local professionals for quality food available in your area. The effort and expense you pay out now will pay you back handsomely in the long run in regard to both health and house-training.

Access to water should be freely given to your dog when he is out of confinement unless he tends to be an excessive drinker. Dogs that abuse their water privileges are few and far between, thank goodness. But if you wind up with a companion (like I currently have) who tends to drink all the water that's available, you may be forced to regulate your dog's access to water.

It is good to note that excessive water drinking can be a sign of a physical problem like diabetes. If your dog drinks water in excessive quantities, be sure to mention it to your vet. In this book, we are assuming that your dog is in good health. Therefore, we are only treating behavioral issues or personality tendencies, not physical maladies when discussing housebreaking or any other training. If ever there is a question of health or concern that there is some physical ailment, stop training immediately and schedule an exam with your veterinarian.

As a general rule of thumb, water can be offered to the dog before or after each elimination opportunity. This is a safe, easy way to make sure your four-legged friend stays well hydrated. The amount of water at each offering can be a slightly trickier calculation. Activity, weather, and the size of the dog all factor in to how much water to offer. I use a visceral approach to regulating my shepherd's intake. Given the time of day (how long since the last drink), current activity (how much panting and heavy breathing), temperature (warmer means more water), I decide so much lapping feels about right. Of course, this is an effortless task for me because I have cared for thousands of dogs under a myriad of conditions. Therefore, I draw from a large sample base as to how much water is optimal at any particular time. The average dog owner, when comparing his excessive drinker to any other dog under similar conditions, should err toward extra water for his buddy (never allowing for a distended stomach) and gradually tweak the amount to just right.

Listening to but not blindly following your feelings during the house-training process is very helpful in establishing a natural flow to the schedule.

Don't be inflexible with the routines if your dog and your gut tell you this is an unusual circumstance.

I would like to discuss a couple of behaviors usually thought of as simple housebreaking issues that really should be handled as problems all their own. We'll cover the more frustrating to deal with first: emotional urination.

This behavior typically is seen in pups and young adults (but can carry over into mature animals) and stems from an inherent tendency in some dogs toward extreme emotional reactions (like excitement or submissiveness) during social greetings. This is an involuntary release of urine on the dog's part and should not be handled with any form of discipline. In fact, correcting or scolding the dog for this reaction only exacerbates the condition. A good handler should never inject strong feelings into an already emotional situation. Our family dog may adhere to all of the house-training rules like a champ and still be an emotional wetter.

Since the emotional urination usually occurs at a precise instant (immediately prior to or the actual moment of touch by a family member, handler, or visitor), our approach to controlling it will be relatively straightforward. A leash and collar will be necessary for the dog at first so we can prevent our canine friend from initiating contact and begin developing in the dog the essential tools needed for self-restraint as laid out in the manners portion of the book.

Having his four-legged friend restrained, the handler is now able to prevent any oncomers from touching his dog until after enough time has elapsed to allow for a return to near normal. Once our friend reaches this near-normal state, a touch from an oncomer is not nearly so significant. Even so, highly stimulating interaction should be discouraged until the dog proves over weeks to months of practice that emotional control in the face of intense social situations is second nature.

The most difficult aspect of emotional urination to overcome is a dog's overreaction to his handler, the one who must touch him to attach the leash and collar, the person first to greet him in the morning or after work, the one who releases him from the crate. In all these cases, the dog is in a high state of excitement and immediate contact is almost unavoidable. If you are the handler faced with this kind of challenge, the only way to minimize and gradually decrease emotional urination is to remove emotion altogether on your part at the initial greeting and reduce physical contact to its barest minimum.

Do not react in any way to the wetting. Attach the leash and collar without delay and whisk your little friend outside where he can relieve himself while normalizing. During this process, don't let your companion abuse you or any rules you've already put in place (leash and collar, for example). Also, to lessen the negativity around the emotional urination issue, arrange your dog's indoor confinement and path to the outdoors in the most convenient manner possible in regards to cleanup (use plastic carpet runners where necessary). Stick to this plan and the involuntary wetting will diminish.

Remember, emotional control is the key to success. Years ago, I worked with a man large in stance but short on patience and his sensitive rottweiler pup. This particular man could not get a grip on his negative reaction to the pup's smallest urinary infraction. Against our advice, this fellow repeatedly chastised and corrected his rottweiler over this involuntary wetting until it worsened to a point that he could no longer tolerate the pup in his house. He eventually took his barely five-month-old companion to the pound.

This case has stuck with me over the years because I can't forget what a bright, handsome pleaser that rott pup was. When this little guy was four months old, he lived at the training center for two weeks while we got his obedience underway. From the start, this happy fellow loved to work, and the little bit of emotional urination we witnessed at the start of his training completely vanished after a week of balanced handling. Tragically, the pup's hot-tempered owner was unable or unwilling to practice even the slightest bit of self-control and eventually became the most potent catalyst for the very behavior he couldn't live with.

The second behavior we need to consider separately from routine housebreaking is territorial marking. The irritating tendency, practiced by both male and female animals, does not stem from a poor housebreaking routine or a lack of bladder control. It is simply a form of graffiti or staking claim: Max lives here, Max was here on someone else's claim, or Max and Zoe are here now trying to spread as much artwork as possible (usually over the other's masterpiece) trying to establish whose claim this actually is.

Territorial marking is generally easy to recognize: frequent, small releases of urine or stool in strategically favorable places (mailboxes, door jams, car tires, couch corners, and, oh yes, owners' legs). So be on high alert, leash and collar on, visual contact established, when you and your dog visit another dog's claim or when a canine visitor comes to your house. Remember, graffiti is all about competition. One artistic mark always, always begets another.

Now that you know the why, where, and when, here is how to deal with territorial marking. As with any other undesirable conduct, the handler needs to deliver a swift and impressive correction as close to the marking action as possible. The deterrent for this behavior must be strong in order to extinguish the overwhelming urge to mark that some dogs possess. With this sort of urination problem, there is no need to follow up with a trip to the proper elimination spot. This is not a bladder issue.

At the training center, we have just under four thousand square feet of indoor instruction space situated on two fenced acres. On an average day, we'll have no fewer than twenty-seven dogs and their owners pass through our doors. Our instructors battle with canine graffiti all week long.

Whether you are in the process of housebreaking a new dog or battling emotional urination or territorial marking, thorough cleanup is necessary to discourage a repeat mistake in the same spot. Every morning at the training center, we make up a fresh mop bucket of bleach and detergent water. We always have on hand a spray bottle of disinfectant and deodorizer. With any mess on hard surfaces, we immediately mop it up and then spray the area down with disinfectant mix and mop again.

On absorbent surfaces, diluting the mess with fresh water and following with generous amounts of fabric or carpet cleaner before blotting with a towel seems to work best. But even with the best effort, only time will reduce the residual odor to a level where a dog will no longer be interested.

My best advice is to take every precaution to minimize eliminations where you don't want them and clean immediately and thoroughly while trying to restrict your dog to hard-surface areas until his training is complete.

Small Dogs

I have a new eight-week-old Pekinese that I am hoping to train as he gets older. Some people say that toy dogs do not do well in obedience training. Is this so? Also, are there things I can do with my Jack Russell puppy that will help him be more accepting of obedience training as he matures?

We have found that toy dogs are no different from other dogs except that they are smaller. Some toy dogs are stubborn, some are aggressive, some are playful, and some are eager to please. They are as varied as the general dog population. They are just smaller and need a lighter touch to achieve the same results.

To get your dog ready for obedience training before he is old enough, consider structured play. Structured play doesn't mean lose the fun. It means that the handler directs the energy and focus of the dog. We are often asked at what age should a person start working with his or her dog? The answer is always the same: *the day you bring him home.* But the intensity of work should always be defined by the dog's age, personality, and the handler's knowledge of dog behavior.

Working with a pup between the ages of eight and sixteen weeks for instance means establishing schedules the pup can count on for sleeping, elimination, and eating. Regular playful interaction is most important work at this age. Games should be productive and can act as preconditioning for more formal training in the future. One of the games we most like to play with our little guys at this age is *follow the leader*. We explore his environment inside and out, making sure to point out things of interest, like bugs and such. Playful retrieve is a fantastic way to exercise your pup while at the same time conditioning him to utility training in the future. Be sure not to turn the retrieve exercise into keep-away (one of those canine skills that always comes back to haunt us). During the retrieve game, use a variety of intriguing items to keep the pup's interest up and entice him to bring you the item he just chased down by tempting him with an item of equal value or food or a game of tug-of-war. Yes, tug-of-war along with wrestling is okay to play, especially at this age. Both are natural forms of interaction and muscle building for dogs, and as long as the handler retains the authority to call a halt to the games, this can be lifelong fun for dog and handler alike.

All of these games endure throughout the relationship, and, as always, consistency establishes the patterns in associating signal to response. Never forget during this game what the final result should be.

If at any time or age the puppy demonstrates genuine aggression during tug-of-war or wrestling, cease and desist with those two games from that point on because the puppy may not possess a temperament suitable for lighthearted combat. Often at the training center, we evaluate pups between the ages of three and six months that are inherently serious in disposition and view the world as a very grave place for no other reason than that nature designed them that way.

Almost without exception, when a family brings us a puppy possessing a severe disposition, the family immediately starts off the session with a disclaimer of no abuse and often points a finger at the breeder for mishandling the puppy prior to the selling age of six to eight weeks.

Although we can empathize with the family's desire to blame someone, in most cases, when we see a young pup who is seriously aggressive or painfully shy, we find that faulty temperament is the culprit. Most of the serious puppies we evaluate show no outward signs of abuse or neglect and in many cases have very concerned owners and breeders looking out for their welfare. So there is no reason for us to assume anything other than the pup's disposition when accounting for this kind of extreme behavior. We also might be dealing with an inherent condition that is a breed-specific tendency.

I want to say a word about breed-specific tendencies. Hunting dogs are hardwired to point. Shepherds herd whatever they can. Newfoundlands are such water dogs that they have webbed feet. Many dogs are bred to emphasize certain tendencies. *However*, having said that, I cannot go on to say that because you have a border collie, you have to have a herd of sheep or the dog will not have a fulfilling life. Dogs, with some few exceptions, can be trained to put aside their tendencies and obey their handlers. Nearly every dog can learn self-control. No dog should be called vicious because she belongs to a breed that might be known for aggression. In nearly every case, a dog's disposition can be shaped by its handler.

At the training center, we evaluate on average about ten dogs and puppies a week. We have seen every imaginable breed type, week in and week out, and we've done this for over two decades. Because of this high volume of temperament evaluations over such an extended period of time, we've had the opportunity to witness definite patterns emerge. For example, we are alert to a number of "red flag" breeds known from past history to possess sharp dispositions, like the explosive aggression of cocker spaniels, chow chows, and Australian shepherds, or the painfully shy and defensive types like German shepherds, Great Danes, and Chihuahuas.

With any dog or pup, regardless of temperament or length of your relationship, an owner can lay an unshakable foundation for recall with come-and-find-me games. One must be somewhat cautious about not being too obsessive with this kind of game; otherwise, some insecurity may develop in your companion over continuously losing his leader.

The truth is the handler doesn't have to disappear from his four-legged friend in order to make this game effective. Simply moving some distance from the pup while he is otherwise engaged and calling him will work beautifully. The key to successful response here is to reward your puppy, give incentives, and keep commands upbeat. The standard reward we offer for this come-and-catch-me game is a hidden treat, which is not exposed or advertised until the dog has reached front and center. With the right canine personality, however, physical affection or a toy will offer just as much incentive to find the handler's front. As always, consistency establishes the patterns in association between the human's signal or command and the canine's response. Use the exact same signal or command during play that you intend to use as your finished directive during formal training. Whenever you initiate this game (which should be, by the way, regularly) don't forget what the final result should be with your formally trained dog (front and center when you call).

Another invaluable game I play with all my dogs is FIND IT, whatever "it" is. Begin with a small treat tossed into the short grass no more than a yard away to ensure success for the beginning puppy. Then steadily advance into toys and objects of all kinds, gradually increasing the scope of the search. Always ensure success and reward for your dog. What a useful skill FIND IT can develop into over the months!

These are just a few of the games that have endured throughout my entire relationship with all my dogs.

One last comment on this foundation building: Be sure to introduce the pup or dog to a buckle collar and leash that he can wear around prior to any handling or playing to help facilitate the proper response without placing too much attention on equipment.

Premature Confidence

My dog has been through obedience training, and we began to walk in an isolated area without a leash. I was really proud of the way Charlie responded until a small herd of deer came into sight down in the valley. Charlie took off like a shot in spite of my calling him, and he didn't return for at least twenty anxious minutes. What did I do wrong?

Trainers beware! All of us at some point or another during dog handling fall victim to a premature sense of training completion. We assume before we should that our dog's way of thinking has come around to our way of thinking. This is especially problematic when dealing with dogs with aggressive behavior or dogs who tend to run off given the opportunity.

Every trainer must allow weeks into months to fully form a dependable habit of response in any dog. To fully shape canine behavior, a person needs to set up numerous successful experiences over a substantial amount of time. We must accept the fact that the dog's true character never changes, so if you begin training a bully or a Houdini, you end your training with a bully or a Houdini. And therein lies the trap: the mistaking of changed behavior for changed character.

Shaping a dog's behavior means changing the way the dog responds to certain stimuli in his environment or adjusting the manner in which a dog reacts in certain situations. Often these changes rub against the dog's natural tendencies and therefore create substantial conflicts within the dog's mind that he must wrestle with and eventually settle, we hope, in favor of a new, more desirable behavior.

As developing human beings, we all know how difficult changing our own habits and behaviors can be. So as dog trainers, we need to be patient and understanding as we gradually shape the behavior of our four-legged friends into more harmonious interaction with the family.

If, as dog trainers, we are successful in supplanting the less desirable original responses with the more desirable new responses, then a new habit has formed, leaving the dog's unique personality intact. Leaving the personality intact means that the dog's natural tendencies toward the old ways still remain, especially in early training.

Remember this shaping process occurs slowly over weeks of reinforcement by consistently linking the appropriate consequences to a specific behavior. And as one can imagine, the stronger a particular dog's personality may be or the more profit (for the dog) associated with a specific behavior, the more challenging shaping is likely to be. So beware of early successes; probably more testing is lying in the wait.

Jealousy

What makes my dog act the way he does? He seems to be jealous of everyone and everything. I am especially worried now that our first baby is coming.

It is greed, not jealousy that drives most dogs. Competition for food, treasures, attention, comfortable places, and leading the way seem to cause families the most grief in raising their dogs.

A family dog's statement of being might be "I'm competing with everyone for everything." This of course is a very natural core value for most living organisms including humans. In primal terms, greed is inextricably linked to survival. So when we evaluate our family dogs and their behavior, for the most part, we must think as the dog thinks in terms of self-preservation and self-gratification. Seen in this light, our dog's behavior is so much easier to understand. And once we understand the dog's basic motivation to act in his own self-interest in most situations, we can develop a plan to adjust the motivation, thereby adjusting the action.

Man's best friend, the opportunist, wants as large a piece of the pie as he can secure. Even though I can't blame him for that, unchecked pie grabbing in a family leads very quickly to anarchy. Someone must become the pie server: you, the trainer. A handler can look at the pie from the canine perspective as anything desirable like food, garbage, attention, best place on the couch, first out the door, or leading the way.

The pie server is in charge of doling out the appropriate-size piece to the appropriate recipient. Period. A dog must be compelled to accept this truth. As good manners and order would dictate, stealing from another recipient is an absolute taboo. Since dogs cannot really measure, and even if they could, would not be allowed to dictate the size of a piece the server hands out, contentment and appreciation rule the day. This is a critical understanding the dog and his handler must come to.

At the training center, we counsel countless expecting families on this idea of greed instead of jealousy and the importance of establishing a pie server to alleviate the worries and difficulties of bringing a new baby home to the family dynamic.

One must remember that our canine companions easily interchange people with dogs in regard to pack rules and order. So carefully establish only two ranks in your family: the privileged rank of all humans, regardless of age, and the subservient rank of all animals, regardless of seniority. The primary handler (pie server) controls all.

I think it's very important to keep in mind when we're dealing with dog behavior that we're dealing with their primal assessments of situations along with their visceral actions. Good dog trainers should work very hard to avoid anthropomorphizing their dogs too much. But at the same time that the handler understands that his dog is not a person, he should keep on the forefront of his mind that a dog is a sentient being. These last three ideas more than any others direct our training approach at the center.

Think of your dog as a primitive being—a nonhuman being, but a feeling being—as you forge your relationship with him and you will not fail in training. All of us dog owners should also keep in mind that our canine companions are unique living beings that we chose to care for.

Dogs are the animals they were meant to be. We should appreciate them for what they are and not what we wish they were. There is a beautiful fable I like telling to illustrate this point. A Native American woman was walking home one day on a familiar path when she came across a wounded rattlesnake. Recognizing the snake as one of God's creations, she took it home to nurse it back to health. After months of care and attention, the rattlesnake once more reached peak condition, so the woman conscientiously returned the snake to the exact place on the path where she found him.

Once on the ground, the snake was so excited to be free and healthy that he wriggled in the dust and slid across the woman's moccasins, catching his tail on some of the beadwork. Instinctively, he reached across to bite his nurturer in the leg. Shocked by his action, the woman asked the snake, "How could you possibly bite me after all the care and attention I've given you?"

The rattlesnake, perplexed by her question, replied simply and honestly, "I feel good. I'm a snake. That's what we do."

The moral of this story: the animal caretaker who expects human rather than creature appreciation for his efforts is the one at fault, not the beast who is acting true to his nature.

Spay/Neuter

I have an unaltered German shepherd who is inclined to be aggressive. I have been told that he would lose that tendency if I were to have him neutered. What do you suggest?

I advocate spaying and neutering programs. Any trip to any animal shelter will make you a believer if you are not already. However, I do not agree with these new, mandatory spay/neuter programs that exist based on the misinformation that spaying/neutering will change the disposition of any dog. There is significant and growing evidence that spaying/neutering will not affect any dog's disposition if the dog is over nine months old.

Often the challenge of dealing with a problem dog centers around aggression and how to control it. At the training center, we manage canine hostility by shaping the behavior of an antagonistic dog to become more docile. By adjusting a dog's reaction to stimulation using the proper forms of motivation, we are able to push the dog toward his genetic potential for adherence and tolerance.

We always work within an individual's limitations, and this sometimes means that environmental conditions need to be modified to reach maximum results and safety. A simple example of this process would be using leash and collar corrections to deter the family dog from barking and growling at a visitor. Once the watchdog has quieted, we pet and praise him for the positive change in his behavior.

If a particular visitor makes the family dog especially uneasy, it may be necessary to put the canine guardian in a designated, secure place to allow both dog and visitor to truly relax. Altering is rarely discussed when dealing with one of these problem cases because the vast majority of these challenging canines were altered prior to our first meeting.

Each dog we evaluate for training is managed as a unique personality, a complex of distinctive traits and characteristics that force us as trainers to deal with them as individuals. What works for one dog in the way of incentives and deterrents may not work at all for another. Dog training, shaping behavior, or modifying a canine's standard response to a stimulus all boils down to motivation. We must give a dog sufficient reason to change his mode of operation.

Spaying and neutering has little or no bearing on the previously described training procedure or its outcome. As stated before, the vast majority of aggressive dogs I work with are altered animals *before* I evaluate them for training.

If on the rare occasion I encounter a volatile canine personality that displays extreme aggressive behavior proving to be an unpredictable danger to handlers and others and who fails to respond favorably to our positive, established training methods, I usually suggest euthanasia for that particular dog, not altering. Considering the 12,000-plus dogs I've worked with over the past twenty-seven years, **I don't recall a single aggressive case where altering the animal neutralized the hostility.**

With proper training and care, the typical, sometimes aggressive, domestic dog can be a socially acceptable member of the human family, serving as companion, assistant, and guardian without eroding the safety of the general public.

Three of the most important responsibilities of every conscientious dog owner in regard to enhancing public safety are primary handler supervision, use of appropriate handling equipment, and secure confinement of the animal when he is not supervised.

By primary handler supervision, I mean that the persons who have developed a positive controlling relationship with a particular dog are the only people qualified to regulate the behavior and whereabouts of that dog.

The appropriate equipment (including but not limited to traffic leads, long lines, slip collars, buckle collars, muzzles, and harnesses) is essential for suitable control over a dog out of his confinement. The length and weight of a particular leash or collar depends entirely on the individual dog being handled, the purpose of the handling, and the conditions of the surrounding environment.

When a dog is securely confined, he must be unable to liberate himself regardless of his determination. The dog must be out of easy reach and release of strangers. Finally, the secure confinement must be hazard-free for the dog. Notwithstanding environmental and budgetary restraints, only the imagination limits the development of truly secure confinements.

I've spent my adult life helping people become better dog owners. By using these three simple responsibilities as guidelines in their daily lives, all pet owners can fully enjoy their pet wherever they go without compromising public safety.

Multiple Dogs in a Household

Help! We got a second dog that we thought would be a good playmate for our four-year-old Lab. Instead, our Lab Mazie has forgotten all of her training and our household is now chaotic. We hate to give our new Lab away, but we can't take much more.

The only way to comfortably control a true pack (more than one) of family dogs is to first establish a solid relationship with each individual based on parameters you lay out for that particular dog. For instance, the Jack Russell in the family may be allowed on the couch with permission from the handler. The family German shepherd, however, is never allowed on the couch. The Jack Russell tends to be restless at night so she sleeps in a crate. The German shepherd, on the other hand, sleeps wherever he wants because he actually sleeps. Both dogs have learned that the German shepherd is usually called to his feed bowl first and the Jack Russell is usually given permission to go outside first.

Just like these casual rules, the rigid parameters of formal commands are set up one dog at a time. Here's what I mean. Prior to the first training session, I choose which dog will begin instruction and attach his leash and collar. The dog or dogs in waiting will then be secured, hopefully within the immediate instruction area in sight of the dog being worked with.

It is critical from the earliest stages of instruction to impress upon the dog in training that the relationship being formed with his handler is in no way affected by the other dogs in the family. Each dog will have his turn with the handler while the others observe. As the days pass and the handler marches through casual manners along with formal commands, unique relationships are forged with each individual. The dogs in waiting should be given more and more freedom to hang out in the training area while instruction continues one on one. By reinforcing good manners in the dogs hanging out, the handler ensures that no one will bother the immediate dog in training. As a side note, all the dogs being supervised or interacted with need to be wearing leashes and collars whether they are in training or in waiting. Those leashes that are not in hand can simply be dragged around by the dogs in sight of the handler, of course.

Do not bite off more than you can chew. For instance, if weeks into this training program, you feel as a conscientious handler that you're capable of managing only one dog at a time, so be it. There is no rush to reach the finished product of controlled family pack. I promise you, rushing means sloppy, fuzzy parameters and loose control over the pack. If dog training is perceived as months' worth of time and energy investment that returns dividends for ten to twelve years, then it becomes much easier for a handler to invest wisely and patiently.

We can't lose sight of the goal, however, which is to develop an easily managed, well controlled, happy family pack. **So, when necessary, recruit help, designate, and instruct a competent person on how to supervise the dogs that are off duty according to the rules you've already set up.** In fact, recruiting a helper from the very onset of training is a great idea. This allows the primary handler to truly concentrate on the dog in hand and clearly demonstrate to the other family members both human and animal. Do not in the least alter the new rules being set up. Dog training should always be a momentum-building process, the human-canine relationship ever gravitating toward the ideal set of interaction rules created by the handler, not the dog.

So in the case of a multiple-dog household, our goal is to end up with the canine family members mingling and interacting with each other, along with their human counterparts, in a mannerly fashion. Our sights are not set simply on a one handler/one dog relationship, so be careful not to contract this exclusive standard only to tear it down and rebuild it within the context of more than one. That's why, at the very start of training if possible, we have some naturally occurring distractions at least on the periphery of the work area.

Consider the advice given to brand-new parents: If you want your child to be able to sleep through normal household activities, make sure normal noises are not quashed when the infant is first introduced to the home.

How is it best to view rank and order among the pack within the human family?

Rank, order, or structure of the pack and family will form one way or another. So as a designated handler, step up to the plate at once and take charge of the pack's direction. If you do not, anarchy among animals and family members will occur and everyone will be sucked into the drama.

Let me lay out the structure of pack and family first. Then I'll walk you through its construction. First of all, I'll tell you that there are only three ranks in a healthy family. The first rank consists of all the humans in the household, regardless of age, size, or handling capabilities. **The second rank is made up of all the dogs in the household, regardless of who came first.** The third rank would be all the other animals in the house along with visitors who will all be treated as guests by the second rank, according to visitor protocol established during basic obedience training.

Order within the ranks flows like this: Among the humans in rank one, the primary dog handler or handlers will obviously stand out to the canine members of rank two. These primary handlers should be, as far as the dogs are concerned, the big boss man and woman, the alphas of their world. Whether these primary handlers are alphas among the human rank is not relevant. But what is important is that somebody in rank one stands out as the controller of rank two. The remainder of the people in rank one can descend in authority from B to Z without undermining the family's social organization, as long as the primary handlers make it perfectly clear that even the lowest in order of rank one is more important than any member of rank two. For instance, a couple's young child toddles up to the couch to squeeze in between Dad and Booger, the beagle. Booger must instantly scoot down the couch and give up his place to the toddler without a complaint. If he does not, it is the primary handler's responsibility to step in and force the beagle to give way, demonstrating that children rank higher than dogs. Although the child's authority is artificial in the sense that the big alpha boss is responsible for the enforcement, the message is still very clear to the dog: If you mess with baby bear, you will have to deal with big bear.

Consistently reinforcing this kind of social family order over a period of months will create a sense of natural compliance and automatic concession on the dog's part to most actions on the child's part. In similar fashion, a non-dog-handling spouse can be given the authority by the primary handling spouse to remove a favorite chew bone from the family dog's possession. In any of these artificial authority situations, it's paramount for safety and success that the primary handler be immediately present and the proper training equipment be used.

As far as order in rank two, that's simple. **All dogs are equal**—at least as far as they view each other's authority. *Do not* allow the well-ensconced eight-year-old family dog to lay down any law to the newly adopted twelve-month-old. By the same token, *do not* allow the newcomer to infringe upon the privileges or comforts of the longtime family member. Remember, the primary handler is in complete charge, no matter what it takes (within reason). So this may mean at first assigning a handler for each dog, utilizing leashes and collars any time the dogs interact with each other, and setting up individual pens for each dog to be used for safekeeping, not punishment.

All these preparations will be necessary to ensure the big boss's rules of social etiquette are followed by all the members of the second rank. If you happen to be a single handler with more than one dog, the leashes, collars, and pens will be of even greater importance when establishing rank and order.

I think it's appropriate to say here that when an owner creates and enforces the rules of social etiquette for the family, he should view the dogs in his group as canine children. From this perspective, an owner can more clearly identify responsibilities for the dogs and more confidently dole out the appropriate consequences for any given canine behavior. For example, most parents would not allow their eight-year-old daughter to spank their four-year-old son for walking too close to her delicate dollhouse. The daughter, more than likely, would be punished for such an act and encouraged the next time to call for an authority figure. Likewise, I doubt many parents would allow their four-year-old son to steal food off his sister's plate at mealtime. It is the parents' job to monitor the behavior of their children and teach through explanation and consequence the appropriate way to interact with siblings, guardians, and guests. So it is with dog owners and their canine children. The only real differences lie with the types of explanations and consequences used for dogs versus children.

Canis familiaris, being genetically wired for pack existence, *needs* not simply wants a clear sense of order within his immediate family. Like an ice cube trying to find its way to the top of the glass, if there is room above, the cubes will compete to fill the space. Left to their own devices, dogs will readily jockey for position of rank, competing with humans and animals alike. In one extreme case I dealt with a few years ago, an elderly couple adopted a young male Lab who grew into a bully. By the time they contacted the training center, the eighty-pound Lab had successfully routed the man out of his own bed. The man retreated to the couch, and the dog slept next to the man's wife. If the husband dared to approach the bedroom or his spouse at bedtime, the confident four-legged alpha would charge the man ferociously sending him to another part of the house. At mealtime, the elderly couple had to lure their eighty-pound boss into the backyard in order to prevent him from taking all the food from their plates.

Although this represents an extreme situation, I deal with milder versions of this unnatural family order every day. Restructuring an existing pack order is very doable, but infinitely more difficult than setting the social rules from the first day the dog enters the home. First impressions are everything with people and dogs when it comes to relationships. So take control of the wheel the moment your canine friend walks onto your property. Set up elimination schedules, feeding times, confinement areas, and exercise regimens.

Introduce your canine companion to collars and leashes right away. Don't delay structured handling like walks on leash, everyday manners, and formal obedience (provided your dog is mature enough). Once a handler has established himself as the controller and put in place the social interaction rules of rank and order, peace will reign in the family with little threat of upset throughout the years.

Why Get a Dog?

One of my children is dying to have a dog. I have seen that dogs are a lot of trouble. Can you tell me the benefits in owning and training and paying the vet bills for a dog?

I told my daughter when she wanted a dog of her own that she could have a dog when she had a job. Owning a dog is for mature, committed people. This is no longer an age when dogs live out in the yard and eat table scraps as they find them. This is an age where people live close together and unattended dogs infringe routinely on the rights of others' property and safety.

This is an age where vet visits are mandatory and where heartworm and flea and tick prevention can take a significant bite out of a family's budget. This is an age where dogs are subject to leash laws and registration laws.

But owning a dog is one of the richest experiences in many people's lives. Owning a dog can lower cholesterol, lower blood pressure, and contribute to faster healing from surgeries and traumatic injuries. Owning a dog to walk with keeps people walking longer. Owning a dog can mean not coming home to an empty house. Owning a dog can mean having something to live for.

I wish each reader the joy of owning a dog. Though owning a dog is expensive and dogs' needs for care are constant, dogs still give back more than they take in their companionship and total loyalty to you. There are very few companions in the world you can say that about!

Training Notes

Training Notes

_____

_____

_____

_____

_____

_____

_____

_____

_____

_____

_____

_____

_____

_____

_____

_____

_____

Training Notes

Training Notes

Training Notes

Training Notes

Training Notes

_____

_____

_____

_____

_____

_____

_____

_____

_____

_____

_____

_____

_____

_____

_____

_____

_____

_____

Training Notes

Training Notes

_____

_____

_____

_____

_____

_____

_____

_____

_____

_____

_____

_____

_____

_____

_____

_____

_____

_____

_____

_____

Training Notes

Made in the USA
Columbia, SC
09 October 2018